Simple Path
to
Wealth

YOUR ROAD MAP TO FINANCIAL INDEPENDENCE

AND A RICH, FREE LIFE

JL COLLINS

jlcollinsnh.com

Cover Design: Carol Chu
Cover Illustration: Trisha Ray
Interior Design: Mary Jaracz

ISBN-10: 1533667926
ISBN-13: 978-1533667922

First Edition
Printed in the United States of America.

DEDICATION

This book is dedicated to my daughter Jessica, for whom it is written and who inspired me to write it. And to the readers of www.jlcollinsnh.com whose questions and comments over the years helped me more fully understand what those aspiring to financial independence want and need to know.

Disclaimer

The ideas, concepts and everything else in this book are simply my opinion based on what has worked for me and what has kicked me in the ass. It may not continue to work for me and it may not work for you.

While I hope the book answers some of your questions and provides valuable guidance, I cannot possibly know the full details of any reader's personal situation or needs.

As the author, I make no representations as to accuracy, completeness, currentness, suitability, or validity of any information in this book and will not be liable for any errors, omissions, or delays in this information or any losses, injuries, or damages arising from its display or use. All information is provided on an as-is basis.

You are solely responsible for your own choices. There are absolutely no guarantees here.

Acknowledgements

I am an avid reader. As such, I have read the acknowledgement page of many books. I've always scoffed. Sure, I'd think to myself, some people might have done a bit to smooth the rough edges, but the real heavy lifting was done by the author who is now just being nice.

Then I wrote this book.

Editing

The Simple Path to Wealth wouldn't exist were it not for my editor, **Tim Lawrence** (www.timjlawrence.com), and that is no idle or simply kind assertion.

His guidance has certainly made the finished product a far better piece. But his relentless encouragement, persistence and faith in the value of and need for the book are what finally dragged me across the finish line. He even relentlessly forced me to pare down my use of the word "relentless" of which I am overly fond. But as he is not editing this acknowledgement page, I get to slip it in again thrice more.

So arduous was this task, near the end he fled for the peace and sanctuary of a monastery. I'm pleased to report, after half a year, he has returned to the rest of us.

Since then he has been living nomadically. Last I heard he was somewhere in Southeast Asia. He writes about adversity and resilience.

Remarkably, he is still speaking to me.

COVER DESIGN

Since the moment I first shared it as a work in progress, the cover of this book has received rave reviews. My guess is you would have given it one too had you been asked. So when I say designer **Carol Chu** (www.heycarolchu.com) did a brilliant job, I do so without fear of contradiction.

Where such talent comes from, who knows? I can tell you, she was a White House intern in the 90s (before Monica Lewinsky's time) and she's burned through three passports; collecting stamps from Haiti, India, Estonia, Japan, France, Denmark, Norway, Finland and Italy along the way. The Russian border patrol once detained her, seizing her passport.

She's been a professional designer for over 15 years and outside of her day job, she's illustrated three books and authored two. She restores and sells mid-century furniture with her poet husband as a side hustle. They met in a blizzard.

All that is well and good, but when it comes to her success with this cover and working with me, my money says the key is that experience with the Russians.

COVER ILLUSTRATION

I love the illustration on this book's cover. I've been friends with **Trisha Ray** (www.trisharay.com) dating back to my bicycle trip thru Ireland where she and her then fiancé kidnapped me, hauled me up to Galway for a music festival and then abandoned me on the side of the road to find my own way back. How could we not wind up friends?

She has lived and worked in twelve countries on four continents and currently resides in New Mexico with her musician partner and a worried cat. Now that she has sold her import/export company, she has more time for her travels with backpack and sketchbook. Her book, *Meanwhile, Back in Los Ranchos*, is filled with her wonderful illustrations and short, well told stories about the adventures that lead to them. "I was arrested twice. Once for reckless parking and once for grave digging. I was guilty of both."

There is even a story, with pictures, about me in there. But not about my kidnapping.

INTERIOR DESIGN

Mary Jaracz has worked as a professional graphic designer for nearly 15 years. She's won awards for her book designs, a rock band T-shirt design, and for her homemade Oreo recipe.

Easily lured into a challenge, she's learned a variety of art forms including glassblowing, ceramics, wood block carving, and fabric design. Mary and her husband enjoy trying to keep up with their late 1800s historic home and their two sons. She can be contacted at maryjaracz@gmail.com.

Should you need the inside of your book designed, or just a good Oreo cookie recipe, I strongly urge you to do so. Assuming, after dealing with me, she ever accepts another assignment.

PROOFREADING

Because I am a bit obsessive, I used two proofreaders. The two I found each had a bit more than just professional proofreading expertise.

- **Dr. Kelly Paradis** has a Ph.D. in atomic physics and currently works as an academic medical physicist at a major medical center in the Midwest. So, of course, when she raised her hand to volunteer I told her she wasn't quite educated enough to proofread *The Simple Path to Wealth*.

  Her graduate work focused on the application of trapped atoms for quantum information and she now applies the principles of physics to treating cancer with radiation therapy, speaking both nationally and internationally about research applications in the field. So, then I figured, "Well, maybe."

In addition to the proofing, she also checked all the math. Probably because she had learned to question my judgement.

When she's not in the lab lighting things on fire or blowing them up, Kelly, her husband, and their cat Apollo write about their own journey to financial independence at www.frugalparadise.com.

- **Rich Carey** is a Lieutenant Colonel in the United States Air Force so, of course, I told him he didn't rank highly enough for this task.

  He has spent most of his 16-year military career overseas. In this time, he has worked with NATO, the United Nations, various foreign militaries and law enforcement organizations, and has even been involved in international peace negotiations. He is fluent in Chinese and also speaks Japanese. More importantly, for my purposes, he is a native English speaker.

  His avocation is financial independence and his approach has allowed him to pay off his D.C. townhouse and student loans in six years. He also has purchased several rental properties which he owns mortgage-free. He writes about his journey at www.richonmoney.com.

FACT CHECKERS

As the concepts, opinions and approaches presented in this book often run counter to the norm, it was especially important to me that the facts be correct. So I used three fact checkers.

Two of the very smartest writers on financial independence out there today are the **Mad Fientist** of www.madfientist.com (a financial blog that includes the occasional travel post) who is still trying to preserve some of his privacy and **Jeremy Jacobson** of www.gocurrycracker.com (a long-term slow travel blog that includes the occasional financial post) who doesn't care.

When I read their work, both these guys routinely have me sitting back in my chair thinking, "Wow. I never thought of that." Or, "I never thought of that in quite that way." When you've been knocking around this investing stuff as long as I have, that's no small thing.

They were just what I needed to keep this book on track.

As was **Matt Becker** of www.momanddadmoney.com. Matt is a fee-only financial planner. As you'll read in the book, I'm a fairly harsh critic of the profession and many in it. But Matt is one of the "good guys" and his insights and perspective have broadened my own. This book is better for it.

READERS

As the book came together, I wanted to make sure it "worked" for my target audience.

What I needed were people who were smart, who loved reading and who knew little about personal finance but who were interested enough to read a book on the subject. I also wanted people who didn't know me personally as to eliminate any bias.

My contacts connected me with three:

- **Tom Mullen** is a globe-trotting Management Consultant and the author of several books on wine, travel and leadership. You can find him, and sample his splendid writing, on www.roundwoodpress.com and www.vino expressions.com.

- As an avid reader, middle school reading specialist and college professor, **Kate Schoedinger** was a perfect choice to read the drafts. She made sure the concepts in this book were clear for the non-financial-types, as she is, in her own wry words, "no financial professor or specialist."

- **Brynne Conroy** is a personal finance blogger and freelance writer. On her site, www.femmefrugality.com, she shares helpful tips and money tricks, largely in the realms of day-to-day savings and increasing income. But she's only recently entered the area of investing, making her a perfect reader for this project. She's smart, knows good writing and enough on the subject to make sure I stayed on track.

FOREWORD

Pete Adeney, a.k.a Mr. Money Mustache (www.mrmoney mustache.com), graciously agreed to write the foreword. Pete is a major force in the world of financial independence and has been a longtime supporter of my blog and investing approach. He is also the first person I asked to be a speaker at our annual Chautauqua event in Ecuador, and he has been there every year since. Those were reason enough to ask him. The fact that he readily agreed and then proceeded to turn out the brilliant piece that follows, is humbling. I owe you, my friend.

EMOTIONAL SUPPORT

Creating this book has been a long and sometimes stressful process. The emotional rollercoaster had me at times depressed, at times foaming-at-the-mouth raving and at times giddy with delight. My wife, **Jane**, endured it all without stabbing me in my sleep. That there is not an award for this is one of the great shortcomings of our civilization.

In short, with all their help, this book is as good as I am able to make it. Any shortcomings, flaws or inaccuracies are entirely mine and very likely result from those few moments when I failed to follow their wise counsel.

Thank you for reading it.

Foreword

There's no shortage of stuff you *really should be learning* in this world, and no shortage of books about exactly that same stuff. Every bit of knowledge you could ever hope for is already waiting right there in a book somewhere. Or a whole shelf of books. Heck, you could probably fill an entire underground parking garage with all the books that have been written on the subject of investing alone, and still find more pouring out onto the ground when you climbed back out.

The problem is that most of those books are boring and you end up setting them down with a bookmark somewhere around page 25, never to return. Even with the best of skills and intentions, I find that the writers of most books about stock investing cannot seem to get it right. They drag it out painfully or write paragraphs so dry and dense that you find yourself re-reading the same passage over and over for half an hour while your mind wanders off to more interesting pastures.

JL Collins takes this old style of investment book writing and disregards it completely. He creates the stuff that your mind wants to run to when it is tired of reading about stocks. Instead of esoteric equations about measuring a stock's *alpha* and comparing it to its *beta*, he compares the entire stock market to a large mug of *beer* and explains why it's still worth buying even when it comes along with an unpredictable quantity of foam.

He lights up the campfire and just starts telling stories, and if those stories just happen to be about exactly what you wanted to learn in the first place, your new knowledge is a happy side effect.

This is exactly what happened in real life a few years ago, when Jim started writing a series of blog posts on www.jlcollinsnh.com about good investing. I read them all as they came out, and they were so good I started referring my own readers to them. The readers liked them so much they referred others. Their numbers reached the thousands, then the hundreds of thousands.

Word kept spreading about the Stock Series, and still does to this day, because it is something people actually enjoy reading. Sure, the author has the technical chops and demonstrates them well in his own enviable financial life. But readers don't keep coming back just to bask in technical wizardry—they are there to enjoy the fire and hear a good story.

I think that amazing response is what motivated Jim to rewrite and expand his great Stock Series into this even-better book. *The Simple Path to Wealth* is a revolutionary book on stock investing (and good finance in general) because you'll actually read it, enjoy it, and then be able to immediately put the lessons profitably into action with your own money.

You'll be relieved to hear that you can be very successful by holding only a single Vanguard fund over your entire lifetime. You can branch out and get a little fancier if you like, but there is nothing to lose, and everything to gain, by keeping things as simple as you can.

Although very few people actually follow it, I have found that the road to a wealthy life really is simple and quite enjoyable to follow, so it only makes sense that a book about it should have those same fine traits. This one does.

Peter Adeney
a.k.a. Mr. Money Mustache
Colorado, June 2016

Table of Contents

BEGINNINGS

---

*"If you reach for a star, you might
not get one. But you won't come up
with a hand full of mud either."*

— Leo Burnett

Chapter I
Introduction

This book grew out of my blog, www.jlcollinsnh.com. The blog, in turn, grew out of a series of letters I had begun to write to my then teenage daughter. These letters concerned various things—mostly about money and investing—she was not yet quite ready to hear.

Since money is the single most powerful tool we have for navigating this complex world we've created, understanding it is critical. If you choose to master it, money becomes a wonderful servant. If you don't, it will surely master you.

"But Dad," my little girl once said to me, "I know money is important. I just don't want to spend my life thinking about it."

For me this was eye-opening. I love this stuff. But most people have better things to do with their precious time than think about money. They have bridges to build, diseases to cure, treaties to negotiate, mountains to climb, technologies to create, children to teach, businesses to open and build.

Unfortunately this benign neglect of things financial leaves you open to the charlatans of the financial world. The people who make investing endlessly complex, because if it can be made complex it becomes more profitable for them, more expensive for us, and we are forced into their waiting arms.

Here's an important truth: Complex investments exist only to profit those who create and sell them. Further, not only are they more costly to the investor, they are less effective.

Here are a few key guidelines to consider:

- Spend less than you earn—invest the surplus—avoid debt.

- Do simply this and you'll wind up rich. Not just in money.

- Carrying debt is as appealing as being covered with leeches and has much the same effect.

- Take out your sharpest knife and start scraping the little bloodsuckers off.

- If your lifestyle matches—or god forbid exceeds—your income, you are no more than a gilded slave.

- Avoid fiscally irresponsible people. Never marry one or otherwise give him or her access to your money.

- Avoid investment advisors. Too many have only their own interests at heart. By the time you know enough to pick a good one, you know enough to handle your finances yourself. It's your money and no one will care for it better than you.

- You own the things you own and they in turn own you.

- Money can buy many things, but nothing more valuable than your freedom.

- Life choices are not always about the money, but you should always be clear about the financial impact of the choices you make.

- Sound investing is not complicated.

- Save a portion of every dollar you earn or that otherwise comes your way.

- The greater the percent of your income you save and invest, the sooner you'll have F-You Money.

- Try saving and investing 50% of your income. With no debt, this is perfectly doable.

- The beauty of a high savings rate is twofold: You learn to live on less even as you have more to invest.

- The stock market is a powerful wealth-building tool and you should be investing in it. But realize the market and the value of your shares will sometimes drop dramatically. This is absolutely normal and to be expected. When it happens, ignore the drops and buy more shares.

- This will be much, much harder than you think. People all around you will panic. The news media will be screaming Sell, Sell, Sell!

- Nobody can predict when these drops will happen, even though the media is filled with those who claim they can. They are delusional, trying to sell you something or both. Ignore them.

- When you can live on 4% of your investments per year, you are financially independent.

What is so simple and clear now I personally had to learn the hard way, and it took decades. Those initial letters to my daughter, then www.jlcollinsnh.com and now this book are all my efforts to share with her what works, where the minefields lie and how simple it all can and should be. My hope is that with it her path will be smoother, her missteps fewer and her own financial freedom will come sooner and with fewer tears.

Now that you've picked up this book, my hope is the same for you. We'll discuss all those bullet points above and more. So let's get started together. We'll begin with a parable.

CHAPTER II
A PARABLE: THE MONK
AND THE MINISTER

Two close boyhood friends grow up and go their separate ways. One becomes a humble monk, the other a rich and powerful minister to the king.

Years later they meet. As they catch up, the portly minister (in his fine robes) takes pity on the thin and shabby monk. Seeking to help, he says:

"You know, if you could learn to cater to the king, you wouldn't have to live on rice and beans."

To which the monk replies:

"If you could learn to live on rice and beans, you wouldn't have to cater to the king."

Most all of us fall somewhere between the two. As for me, it is better to be closer to the monk.

Chapter III

My story: It has never been about retirement

For me, the pursuit of financial independence has never been about retirement. I like working and I've enjoyed my career. It's been about having options. It's been about being able to say "no." It's been about having F-You Money and the freedom it provides.

I started working when I was 13; even earlier if you count selling flyswatters door-to-door and collecting pop bottles from the side of the road for the deposits. For the most part, I've enjoyed work and I've always loved being paid.

From the beginning, I was a natural saver. Watching my money grow was intoxicating. I've never been sure how this started. It might be hardwired into my genes. It might be my mother seducing me with the image of the red convertible I'd be able to buy when I turned 16. But that was not to be.

My father's health failed before that birthday and shortly thereafter so did his business. My savings went to pay for college and I learned it is a fiscally insecure world. Convertibles came later. To this day it stuns me to read about some middle-aged guy laid off from his job of twenty years and almost instantly broke. How does anyone let that happen? It is the result of failing to master money.

Long before I heard the term, I knew I wanted F-You Money. If memory serves, the phrase originates in James Clavell's novel

Noble House, and from the moment I read it, my goal had a tangible form and an unforgettable name.

In the novel, a young woman is on a quest to secure her own "F-You Money." By this, she means enough money to be completely free of the demands of others and able to do exactly what she wants with her life and time. She's after 10 million, far more than it takes to reach simple financial independence. At least for me. It helps to have a bit of the monk inside.

The other thing I quickly figured out is that financial independence is at least as much about being able to live modestly as it is about cash, as our opening parable describes.

Unlike in the novel, for me enough F-You Money isn't necessarily enough to live on for the rest of your life. Sometimes it's only just enough to step to the side for a while. I first had mine at age 25 when I'd managed to save the princely sum of $5,000; something achieved after working two years at $10,000 per year.

It was my first "professional" job and it had taken me two long post-college years supporting myself doing minimum wage grunt work to find it. But I wanted to travel. I wanted to spend a few months bumming around Europe. I went to my boss and asked for four months of unpaid leave. Such a thing was unheard of in those days. He said "no."

Back then I had no idea that working relationships were negotiable. You asked. Your employer decided and answered. Done.

I went home and spent a week or so thinking about it. In the end, as much as I liked the job and as tough as I assumed finding another would be, I resigned. I wanted to go to Europe. Then a funny thing happened. My boss said, "Don't do anything rash. Let me talk to the owner."

When the dust settled, we agreed on a six-week leave which I spent riding my bicycle around Ireland and Wales.

While I might not have initially realized such things could be negotiated, I learned quickly enough. I also asked for and received a month of annual vacation going forward. That got me to Greece the following year. My eyes were opened. F-You Money not only paid for the trip, it bought me room to negotiate. I'd never be a slave again.

Since then, I've quit jobs four more times and have been kicked to the curb once. I've sat on the sidelines for as little as three months and for as long as five years. I've done it to change careers, to focus on buying a business, to travel and—the time it wasn't my call—with no plan at all. I did it most recently in 2011 and the intention this time is to remain retired. But who knows? I do like getting paid.

My daughter was born during one of these, ahem, unpaid leaves. These things happen when you have time on your hands. Now an adult, she has grown up with anything from dad working 18-hour days and constantly away from home, to dad sleeping late and lounging around. But she always knew that I was doing, for the most part, exactly what I wanted to do at the time.

I like to think that these experiences taught her the value of having money and the joy of work when you aren't effectively a slave to it.

When she was about two, her mom went back to school. This was during my business-buying phase and I had lots of free time.

While Mom was at the university in the evenings, my daughter and I spent endless hours watching *The Lion King* over and over. And over. I've probably seen that movie more times than all other movies combined. We still laugh remembering the teacup towers and Lincoln Log cabins we built. These hours were the foundation of the relationship we've grown to cherish.

Even though I didn't have a paycheck coming in at the time, we also decided my wife should quit her job to become a stay-at-home mom. While she liked the idea, this was a very tough call for her. Like me, she'd been working since childhood and loved it. She felt that without a job, she wouldn't be contributing.

"We have F-You Money," I said. "We don't care about fancy cars or a bigger house. If you kept working what could we possibly buy with the money that would have more value than you being home with our daughter?"

Put in those terms, the choice was easy. She quit. It was far and away the best "purchase" we ever made. Of course, this also meant we had no working income. However, for the three years we both weren't working, our net worth actually grew. It was the first time we fully realized we had moved beyond just having F-You Money. We had become financially independent.

As for me, I failed in finding a business to buy though the search morphed into consulting work and a couple of years into that a client hired me for more money than I'd been making at the job I'd left years earlier. Such is the price of failure in the U.S.

When we moved to New Hampshire, my wife volunteered in our daughter's grammar school library. Their hours, of course, matched perfectly. After a couple of years the school offered her a paid gig. It wasn't the corporate job she'd been used to, but it was also stress-free and fun. She's never looked back.

For the most part, over the 34 years we've been married at least one of us has been working. That handily solved the tough problem of health insurance. During the early 1990s, when we had an overlapping employer-less few years, we bought a high deductible catastrophic health plan. It is too long ago to remember the details and they likely wouldn't apply today anyway. But that's what we'll seek out if and when my wife decides to hang it up before we hit 65 and Medicare. For now, she loves working with the kids at her school and the time off it allows her for our traveling.

As I'll detail later in the book, and as its title implies, our investments are the soul of simplicity.

You'll also see I'm not a fan of the "multiple income stream" school of investing. Simple is, in my book (pun intended), better. So we have no cattle, gold, annuities, royalties and the like.

When I quit work in 2011 and we fully settled into our financial independence, we still had a couple of leftover investments from earlier times. These represented the last remnants of the many investing mistakes I've made over the years. Now in retirement, we've burned those up first as we needed the cash. They mostly revolved around the idea that I could pick investments that would outperform the basic stock index. It took me far too long to accept just how impossibly difficult a task that is. Three things saved us:

1. Our unwavering 50% savings rate.
2. Avoiding debt. We've never even had a car payment.
3. Finally embracing the indexing lessons Jack Bogle—the founder of The Vanguard Group and the inventor of index funds—perfected 40 years ago.

Looking back, what is striking to me is how many mistakes I've made along the way. Yet those three simple things got us to where we wanted to be. That should be encouraging to anyone out there who has also made poor choices along the way and who is ready to change.

When my journey began, I knew no one else following such a path. I had no idea where it would or could lead. I had no one to tell me stock picking was a sucker's game or that swinging for the fences isn't needed to reach financial independence. That last point alone would have saved me the $50,000 of my money Mariah International (a gold mining penny stock) burned through while failing, and failing to make me rich.

So now I'm (again) retired and it feels great. I love not having to keep regular hours. I can stay up till 4 am and sleep till noon. Or I can get up at 4:30 and watch the sun rise. I can ride my motorbike any time the weather or my pals beckon. I can hang around New Hampshire or disappear for months at a time to South America. I post on my blog when the spirit moves me and I might even get another book or two written. Or I can just sit on the porch with a cup of coffee and read the books others have written.

One of my very few regrets is that I spent far too much time worrying about how things might work out. It's a huge waste, but it is a bit hardwired into me. Don't do it.

The older I get the more I hold each day precious. I've become steadily more relentless in purging from my life things, activities and people who no longer add value while seeking out and adding those that do.

It's a big beautiful world out there. Money is a small part of it. But F-You Money buys you the freedom, resources and time to explore it on your own terms. Retired or not. Enjoy your journey.

But first, please be sure to carefully read the important notes that follow.

Chapter IV

Important notes

Note #1: Things change

At some points in this book, I've cited various laws and regulations, and used specific numbers for things like the expense ratios of mutual funds, tax brackets, limits on contributions to investment accounts and the like. While these were all accurate at the time of writing, like many things in this world they are subject to change. Indeed, frequently during the various rewrites of the manuscript I found myself having to update them.

By the time you read this book, some will surely be out-of-date. As they are used primarily to illustrate the broader concepts I am presenting, this shouldn't matter much. However, if you find for your situation or even just for your own curiosity it does, by all means take the time to look up the most current rules and numbers for yourself.

Note #2: On the projections and calculators used in this book

In Chapters 3, 6, 13, 19, 22 and 23 you will find various "what if" scenarios.

In creating these, I had first to select a given calculator and then the parameters to enter. By definition, this means these scenarios are only for the purpose of making or demonstrating a point. While the data and input are accurate, the results are not, and cannot be, a prediction of what the future will hold.

In each case, the URL for the calculator used is provided along with the settings chosen. For example:

* http://dqydj.net/sp-500-return-calculator/
  (Use: Dividends reinvested/ignore inflation)
** http://dqydj.net/sp-500-dividend-reinvestment-and-periodic-investment-calculator/
  (Click "Show Advanced" and check "Ignore Taxes" and "Ignore Fees")
*** http://www.calculator.net/investment-calculator.html
  (Click "End Amount" tab)

In running these scenarios, I chose:

• To select "Dividends reinvested" because this is typically what investors do (and should do) while investing to build their wealth.
• To ignore inflation (too unpredictable), taxes (too variable between individuals) and fees (also variable and if you choose the index funds I recommend, minimal).

If you want to see what the numbers look like including any of these variables, I encourage you to visit the calculators and run the numbers with your own specifications.

Most often in running these scenarios, the period of time I've chosen has been January 1975 - January 2015, for these reasons:

• It is a nice, solid 40-year period and this book advocates investing for the long term.

- 1975 is the year Jack Bogle launched the world's first index fund and this book advocates investing in index funds.
- 1975 happens to be the year I started investing, not that this matters to you.

As it happens, from January 1975 - January 2015, using the parameters I chose above, the market returned an average of 11.9% per year. As you'll learn reading this book, the actual returns for any given year were all over the place. But when the dust settled, over that 40-year period, the average was 11.9%.

That is a breathtaking number.

Already I can hear the naysayers howling: From January 2000 - January 2009 the market wasn't returning anywhere near 11.9%. True enough. Returns then were an ugly -3.8% with dividends reinvested. But that time frame encompassed one of the very worst investment periods of the last 100 years.

During one of the best, January 1982 - January 2000, returns blew past 11.9%; averaging around 18.5% per year. More recently, since January 2009 until January 2015 the return has been 17.7% per year.

The fact is, in any given year, it is exceedingly rare that the market will deliver any specific return. Moreover, the average market return will vary dramatically depending on exactly what period you choose to measure.

So, this left me with a bit of a dilemma. The real, actual return for that 40-year period was 11.9%. But, and let me be absolutely clear about this, *in no way should it be used as an expected return going forward.*

I am NOT for a moment suggesting that you can count on 11.9% annual returns in planning for your future.

The idea that someone might think I am gave me serious pause.

So I considered using a different time span. But given the variables above, that would only project a different percentage equally unlikely to hold going forward.

Using the same 40-year span but with different parameters was an option. Those results look like this:

- Without reinvesting dividends: 8.7%
- Without reinvesting dividends + inflation: 4.7%
- Reinvesting dividends + inflation: 7.8%

But for the reasons mentioned above these seemed even less useful, even if less shocking.

I briefly considered just using a random percentage that seemed reasonable, say 8%. Indeed, as you'll see, I do use 8% in a couple of illustrations. It is commonly said the market returns between 8-12% annually and for those cases using the lower end of that range seemed most reasonable. But still that's just pulling a number out of the air and who is to say what's "reasonable"?

In the end, as you'll see, I mostly went with the breathtaking 11.9%. As they say, it is what it is. But, and again,...

I am NOT for a moment suggesting that
you can count on 11.9% annual returns in
planning for your future.

We are only doing a bit of "what-if" analysis here to explore the possibilities. If 11.9% strikes you as too high—or too modest—you can run the numbers using the percentage or time period that seems most reasonable to you.

Whatever you choose, it won't be what happens each year even if it turns out to be reasonably correct in measuring the decades. Nobody can predict the future precisely, and that's something to remember any time you are looking at exercises such as these.

PART 1:

ORIENTATION

"The tide is high but I'm holding on."
—Blondie

Chapter 1

Debt: The Unacceptable Burden

A couple of years after I was out of college, I got my first credit card. They were tougher to come by in those days. Not like now when my unemployed pet poodle has his own line of credit.

The first month I racked up about $300 or so. When the bill came, there was each charge listed by vendor, with the total at the bottom. In the upper right-hand corner there was a box with a $ sign in it and a blank space beside it. Under this in bold letters it read: Minimum payment due: $10.

I could hardly believe my eyes. I get to buy $300 worth of stuff and they only require me to pay them back $10 a month? And I can still buy more? Wow! This is awesome!

But still, in the back of my mind I could hear my father's voice: "If it sounds too good to be true, it is." Not "it could be" or "it might be." It is.

Fortunately, my older sister was sitting nearby. She pointed out the fine print. The part about them planning to charge me 18% interest on the $290 they were hoping I'd let ride. What? Did these people think I was stupid!?

As a matter of fact they did. It was nothing personal. They think the same of all of us. And unfortunately, all too frequently they're not wrong.

Pause for a moment and take a look at the people around you, literally and figuratively.

What you'll often see, if you scratch the surface just a bit, is an unquestioning acceptance of the single most dangerous obstacle to building wealth: Debt.

For marketers, it is a powerful tool. It allows them to sell their products and services far more easily, and for far more money, than if it didn't exist.

Do you think the average cost of a new car would be pushing $32,000 without E-Z financing? Or that a college education would cost over $100,000 if it were not for readily available student loans? Think again.

Not surprisingly, debt has been promoted as, and largely embraced as, a perfectly normal part of life.

Indeed, it is hard to argue that it has not become "normal." As I write, here in the U.S. Americans carry a total debt burden of ~12 trillion dollars:

- ~8 trillion in home mortgages.
- ~1 trillion in student loans.
- ~3 trillion in other consumer loans such as credit card debt and auto loans.

By the time you read this, these numbers will undoubtedly be higher. And most disturbingly, almost no one you know will see this as a problem. In fact, most will see it as their ticket into the "good life."

But let's be clear. This book is about guiding you towards financial independence. It is about buying your financial freedom. It is about helping you become wealthy and putting you in control of your financial destiny.

Look around at those people again. Most will never achieve this, and their acceptance of debt is the single biggest reason why.

If you intend to achieve financial freedom, you are going to have to think differently. It starts by recognizing that debt should not be considered normal. It should be recognized as the vicious, pernicious destroyer of wealth-building potential it truly is. It has no place in your financial life.

The idea that many (indeed most) people seem to happily bury themselves in debt is so beyond my understanding it is hard to imagine how, let alone why, the downsides would need be explained. But here are a few:

- Your lifestyle is diminished. Set aside any aspirations to financial freedom. Even if your goal is living the maximum consumer lifestyle, the more debt you carry the more of your income is devoured by interest payments. A (sometimes huge) portion of your income has already been spent.
- You are enslaved to whatever source of income you have. Your debt needs to be serviced. Your practical ability to make choices congruent with your values and long-term goals is seriously constrained.
- Your stress levels build. It feels as if you are being buried alive. The emotional and psychological effects of being saddled with debt are real and dangerous.
- You endure the same type of negative emotions experienced by any addict: shame, guilt, loneliness, and above all, helplessness. The fact that it's a prison of your own making makes it all the more difficult.
- Your options can become so narrowed and your stress levels so high, you risk turning to self-destructive patterns

that only reinforce the dependence on spending. Drinking perhaps, or smoking. Or, ironically, shopping and still more spending. It's a dangerous, self-perpetuating cycle.

- Your debt tends to focus your attention on the past, present and future exclusively in the worst possible way. You become fixated on your past mistakes, your present pain and the disaster looming ahead.

- Your brain tends to shut down on the subject with the vague hope it will all resolve itself in some magical way and in the magical time of later. Living with debt becomes hardwired in your financial attitudes, habits and values.

OK, BUT WHAT DO I DO ABOUT THE DEBT I HAVE?

While the mantra here is "avoid debt at all costs," if you already have it, it is worth considering if paying it off ahead of schedule is the best use of your capital. In today's environment, here's my rough guideline:

If your interest rate is...

- Less than 3%, pay it off slowly and route the money to your investments instead.
- Between 3-5%, do whatever feels most comfortable: Either put the money to debt payment or investments.
- More than 5%, pay it off ASAP.

But this is just looking at the numbers. There is a lot to be said for focusing on just getting it out of your life and moving on. Especially if keeping your debt under control has been a problem for you.

OK, I'm gonna pay it off! What now?

Countless articles and books have been written about ridding yourself of debt. If after reading this chapter you feel you need more guidance and help, by all means embrace them. But be careful not to let the pursuit of the *methods* get in the way of the *doing*. The truth is, there is no easy way. But it is pretty simple.

Here's what I'd do:

- Make a list of all your debts.
- Eliminate all non-essential spending, and I mean all of it. Those routine $5 coffees, $20 dinners and $12 cocktails add up. This is what will free up the money you need to pour on the debt flames that are burning up your life. The more you pour, the sooner you stop burning.
- Rank your debts by interest rate.
- Pay the minimum required on all your debts and then focus the rest of your available money on the one with the highest interest rate first.
- Once you've blown that one away, move on to the second highest and right on down the list.
- Once you're done, send me a note and let me know. I'll be raising my glass in a kudos salute to you!

Here's what I would *not* do:

- I would *not* pay a service to help. This only adds to your cost and such credit counseling services have no magic formulas or techniques to make this less painful. You, and only you, can do the work.
- I would *not* worry about trying to consolidate your loans into one place, not even for a lower interest rate. You are going to pay these puppies off fast and hard. Once they're gone

your interest rate will be *Zero*. That's your goal, not merely taking your rate from 18% to 12%. Focus your time and attention there, rather than on exploring clever strategies.

- I would *not* pay off the smaller loans first for the psychological boost. I know this is a key part of at least one popular strategy, and if it makes you more likely to stay the course, so be it. But as you'll learn reading further in this book, I'm not a fan of such crutches. Better to adapt yourself and your attitudes to the numbers than to adapt the strategies to your psychological comfort levels.

In short, nothing fancy. Just do the work and get it done.

This is not going to be easy. Simple, yes. Easy, no.

It will require you to rather dramatically adjust your lifestyle and spending to free up the money you need to direct toward your debt.

It will require serious discipline to stay the course over the months, maybe years, it will take to eliminate your debt.

But here's the good news, and it really is *awesomely* good:

Once you've ingrained that lower spending lifestyle and made diverting the excess cash to your debt your path, you will have also created exactly the platform required to begin building your financial independence.

Once the debt is gone, you need only shift the money to investments.

Where once you had the satisfaction of watching your debt diminish, you'll now have the joy of watching your wealth build.

Waste no time. Debt is a crisis that needs immediate attention. If you are currently in debt, paying it off is your top priority. Nothing else is more important.

Look again at those people around you. For most, debt is simply a part of life. But it doesn't have to be for you.

You weren't born to be a slave.

A FEW CAUTIONARY WORDS ON "GOOD DEBT."

Occasionally you will hear the term "good debt." Be very cautious when you do. Let's briefly look at the three most common types.

Business loans

Some (but not all) businesses routinely borrow money for any number of reasons: acquiring assets, financing inventory and expansion to name a few. Used wisely, such debt can move a business forward and provide greater returns.

But debt is always a dangerous tool and the history of commerce is littered with failed companies ruined by the debt they took on.

Astutely dealing with such debt is beyond the scope of this book, other than to say those who use it successfully do so with great care.

Mortgage loans

Taking on a mortgage to buy a house is the classic definition of "good debt." But don't be so sure.

The easy availability of mortgage loans tempts far too many into buying houses they don't need or that are far more expensive than prudent. Shamefully, this overspending is often encouraged by real estate agents and mortgage brokers.

If your goal is financial independence, it is also to hold as little debt as possible. This means you'll seek *the least house to meet your needs rather than the most house you can technically afford.*

Remember, the more house you buy, the greater its cost. Not just in higher mortgage payments, but also in higher real estate taxes, insurance, utilities, maintenance and repairs, landscaping, remodeling, furnishing and opportunity costs on all the money tied up as you build equity. To name a few.

More house also means more stuff to maintain and fill it. The more and greater things you allow in your life, the more of your time, money and life energy they demand.

Houses are an expensive indulgence, not an investment. That's OK if and when the time for such an indulgence comes. I've owned them myself. But don't let yourself be blinded by the idea that owning one is necessary, always financially sound and automatically justifies taking on this "good debt."

Student loans

When I was in college at the University of Illinois from 1968-72, the total annual cost was $1,200. This $1,200 covered everything: tuition, books, rent, food and even a little entertainment.

Each 12-week summer I worked taking down diseased Elm trees. I was paid $20 a day over a six-day week. I saved $100 a week and by fall had the $1,200 needed for the school year.

Of course, I lived in one room of a dilapidated old house that should have been condemned. White rice and ketchup were served as dinner two or three times a week.

Fast-forward to 2010-14, my daughter's college years. The all-in yearly cost averaged $40,000 at the University of Rhode Island, also a state school. New York University, her other option, would have run ~$60,000 per year. As a former colleague of mine once said, that's like buying a new BMW, driving it for a year and throwing it away. Then buying another. For four consecutive years.

Inflation certainly played a role. Using the CPI (consumer price index), what cost $1 in 1970 took $6.19 to buy in 2014. A six-fold increase.

In the same time period, a 4-year state school college education went from $4,800 to $160,000. A 33-fold increase.

Make no mistake: Easily obtained student loans have flooded the system with money.

Universities have been and continue on a building boom. Fancier prices require fancier settings.

The average salary of a university president in 1970 was ~$25-30,000. Today it averages around $500,000 and can run into the millions.

Not only has this driven up the cost of everything college related, it has effectively eliminated the option of living cheaply.

That ramshackle house I lived in? Torn down to make way for fancy new dorms.

Eat in on rice and ketchup? No worries, my friends did the same. It was a source of pride. Today, it would be a source of embarrassment as all your student loan funded pals go out for sushi.

Moreover, one of the more unfortunate results of spiraling college costs and debt is the way it has warped the very concept of higher education. Rather than the pursuit of learning and culture, it has become the pursuit of job training in an effort to secure employment that will justify the astounding cost and debt incurred.

Even successfully applied, this shackles young people to jobs long after the appeal has faded. Youth should be spent exploring—building and expanding one's horizons—not grinding away in chains.

Here's the real kicker: Unlike other kinds of debt, as truly awful as they are, you can never walk away from your student loans.

They survive bankruptcy. They will follow you to your grave. Your wages, and even Social Security, can be garnished to pay them.

No wonder banks are falling all over themselves to issue this debt.

I am a firm believer in personal responsibility and that debts freely taken on should be faithfully repaid. But the ethics of encouraging 17 and 18-year-olds—who likely have little financial savvy—to almost automatically accept this burden give me serious pause.

We are creating a generation of indentured servants. It's hard to see the ethics or benefits in that.

CHAPTER 2
WHY YOU NEED F-YOU MONEY

Shortly after 9/11 my company kicked me to the curb.

Six months earlier our division president had taken me to a congratulatory lunch for a record-breaking year. We were growing explosively and embarrassingly profitable. Over a bottle of fine wine we discussed my very bright future.

It was the best job I've ever had. We had a great team, great leadership, great fun, and I made great money. I had just cashed a bonus check for more than I had ever made in a single year before.

A year later, my little girl and I were sitting on the couch watching a news broadcast. The concerned news crew was filming people standing in a depression-era style bread line. They were, the reporter said, the newly poor suffering from job loss in the dismal economy. I was still unemployed and licking my wounds.

"Daddy," said my then eight-year-old, "are we poor?" She was gravely concerned.

"No," I said, "we're just fine."

"But you don't have a job," she said. She was thinking, I'm sure, just like those poor jobless souls on the TV. Who even thought she knew what a job was?

"That's no problem, honey. We have money that's working for us instead."

That's what I said, but what I was thinking was: This was exactly why I had worked so hard to be sure I had F-You Money. In fact I'd been working on it long before I heard the term.

I may not have known at first what it was called, but I knew what it was and why it was important. There are many things money can buy, but the most valuable of all is freedom. Freedom to do what you want and to work for whom you respect.

Those who live paycheck to paycheck are slaves. Those who carry debt are slaves with even stouter shackles. Don't think for a moment that their masters aren't aware of it.

As already described, I first accumulated the modest amount of F-You Money I needed to negotiate extra vacation time two years into my first professional job. By 1989 the amount and the freedom it provided had grown substantially. Not enough to retire, perhaps, but easily enough to say F-you if needed.

The timing was fortunate. I wanted to take some time off to pursue business acquisitions. When one morning I found myself and my boss in the office hallway screaming at each other, it occurred to me perhaps the time had come.

I may not have owned a Mercedes, but I owned my freedom. Freedom to choose when to leave a job and freedom from worry when the choice wasn't mine.

Good thing. It turned out I was unemployed for three full years after 9/11. I'm really lousy at job hunting.

Chapter 3

Can everyone really retire a millionaire?

"I wonder if it would actually be possible for every single person to retire a millionaire?"

That very provocative question was posed on my blog a few years back. It's been rattling around in my brain ever since.

The short answer is a qualified "Yes!" it is possible for every middle class wage earner to retire a millionaire. Though it's never going to happen. And that's not because the numbers don't work.

The numbers tell us that, compounded over time, it actually takes very little money invested to grow to $1,000,000. Over the 40 years from January 1975 - January 2015 the market has averaged an annual return of ~11.9% with dividends reinvested (~8.7% if you spent your dividends along the way).* At that rate just $12,000 invested in the S&P 500 stocks in 1975 would be worth over a cool million ($1,077,485) today.**

Don't have $12,000 lying around? That's OK. If you started in January 1975 and invested $130 per month ($1,560 a year) by

---

*   http://dqydj.net/sp-500-return-calculator/
       (Use: Dividends reinvested/ignore inflation)

**   http://dqydj.net/sp-500-dividend-reinvestment-and-periodic-
       investment-calculator/
       (Click "Show Advanced" and check "Ignore Taxes" and "Ignore Fees")

January 2015 you would have had $985,102.** Not quite a million, but not a hand full of mud either.

Want nothing less than the full million? Kicking it up an extra $20 to $150 per month—or $1,800 a year—would have gotten you to $1,136,656.** Your million plus a new Tesla and Corvette.

If you think about it, this is pretty amazing considering all the financial turmoil of the past 40 years. However, it's important to know that compounding takes time, so it helps to start young.

Of course, a million dollars is a very arbitrary goal. Perhaps the better question is: Can everybody achieve financial independence?

On blogs like www.earlyretirementextreme.com and www.mrmoneymustache.com, you'll find countless stories of people with modest incomes who by way of frugal living and dedicated savings get there in a remarkably short time. For example, if you can live on $7,000 per year as the author of Early Retirement Extreme contentedly does, $175,000 gets it done figuring an annual withdrawal rate of 4%. (See Chapter 29)

On the other hand, I remember having lunch with a friend of mine in 1995 shortly before Christmas. He'd just gotten his annual bonus: $800,000. He spent the lunch complaining that it simply wasn't possible to make ends meet with just a lousy *eight hundred thousand dollar* year-end bonus. Somewhat stunningly, listening to him list his expenses, he was right. He was burning through more than $175,000 every three months. Financial independence was a distant dream for him.

** http://dqydj.net/sp-500-dividend-reinvestment-and-periodic-investment-calculator/
(Click "Show Advanced" and check "Ignore Taxes" and "Ignore Fees")

Money is a very relative thing. Right now I have roughly $100 in my wallet. For some (very wealthy) people out there, $10,000 has less relative value to their net worth. For (even wealthier) others, it's $100,000. For still others (the vast number of very poor in the world), $100 might be more than they'll see in an entire year.

Being independently wealthy is every bit as much about limiting needs as it is about how much money you have. It has less to do with how much you earn—high-income earners often go broke while low-income earners get there—than what you value. Money can buy many things, none of which is more important than your financial independence. Here's the simple formula:

Spend less than you earn—invest the surplus—avoid debt

As we discussed in the introduction, do only this and you'll wind up rich. Not just in money. But if your lifestyle matches or exceeds your income, you forfeit your hopes of financial independence.

Let's consider an example. Suppose you make $25,000 per year and you decide you want to be financially independent. Using some of the lifestyle tips from the blogs above, you'd want to organize your life in such a fashion as to live on $12,500 annually. Two important things would immediately happen. You'd have reduced your needs and created a source of cash with which to invest. Now let's use our calculators to play with some scenarios.

Assuming you'll be financially independent when you can live on 4% of your net worth each year, you'll need $312,500 ($312,500 x 4% = $12,500). Investing your $12,500 each year (We'd invest in VTSAX—Vanguard's Total Stock Market Index

Fund) and assuming the 11.9% annual return of the market over the last 40 years, you are there ($317,175) in ~11.5 years.***

At this point suppose you say, "OK I'm done with saving and I'm going to double my spending and spend my full earned $25,000 from now on. But I'll leave my $312,500 nest egg alone." In 10 short years it will have grown to $961,946*** without you having to add a single dime. That amount yields $38,478 a year at a 4% withdrawal rate. You can now not only quit working, you can give yourself a (rather substantial) raise.

For the sake of simplicity, I've ignored taxes at this point. However, I've also assumed you'll never see an increase in income. Plus, I've tossed in VTSAX and 4% withdrawal rates. Don't worry, we'll look at those in depth a bit later. For now, we're just doing a bit of "what if" analysis to help you see that your money can buy you something far more valuable than stuff.

Unfortunately, few will ever even see this as an option. There are pervasive and powerful marketing forces at work seeking to obscure the idea that such a choice exists. We are relentlessly bombarded with messages telling us that we absolutely need the latest trinket and that we simply must have the most fashionable of currently trending trash. We're told that if you don't have the money, no problem. That's what credit cards and payday loans are for.

It is this thinking that makes it so hard for most people to see that it is possible to reach a million dollar net worth on an income of $25,000. This is not some evil conspiracy at work. It is simply business pursuing its own needs. But it is deadly to your wealth.

The science behind the art of this persuasion is truly impressive, and the financial stakes are huge. The lines between need and want are continually and intentionally blurred. Years ago, a

---

*** http://www.calculator.net/investment-calculator.html
(Click "End Amount" tab)

pal of mine had bought a new video camera. It was the best of the best and he was filming every moment of his young son's life. In a burst of enthusiasm he said: "You know, Jim, you just can't raise a child properly without one of these!"

Ah, no. Actually you can. In fact, billions of children have been raised over the course of human history without ever having been videotaped. And horrific as it may sound, many still are today. Including my own.

You don't have to go far to meet someone who will tell you about all the things they can't live without. You likely know your share of people like this. But if you want to be wealthy—both by controlling your needs and expanding your assets—it pays to reexamine and question those beliefs.

Chapter 4

How to think
about money

Level 1: It's not just about spending

Get yourself a nice, crisp one of these:

Now prop it up on the table in front of you and give some thought as to what it means to you. For instance…

1. You might think about what you could buy with it right now. One hundred dollars buys a very nice dinner for two at a good restaurant. A fancy pair of sneakers. A tank of gas for your big-ass pick'em up truck. A few bags of groceries. Maybe a nice sweater? I dunno. I don't buy much stuff, so this is hard for me. I did just buy a $119 L.L. Bean bed for my dog. It's going back. He won't sleep in it.

2. You might think, Mmmm...I could invest this money. Historically the stock market returns somewhere between 8-12% a year on average. I could spend that each year and still always have my $100 earning more for me.

3. You might think, but inflation and market drops are a concern. I'll invest my $100 but only spend 4% a year. Any extra earnings I'll re-invest so my $100 grows and the money it throws off keeps pace with inflation.

4. You might think, I'll invest this money and I'll re-invest what it earns and then re-invest what that earns, and years from now, after the power of compounding has worked its magic, I'll think about spending it.

You can probably come up with other variations, but looking at these it's easy to see that one view will keep you poor, one will get you into the middle class, one will take that a step further and the last will make you rich.

Consider Mike Tyson

Mr. Tyson was one of the most intimidating and formidable boxers of all time. Few have mastered the "Sweet Science" (boxing) better. The "Dismal Science" (economics)—not so much. After earning some $300,000,000, he wound up bankrupt. A lifestyle reputed to cost $400,000 a month didn't help. And as is always the case with the suddenly wealthy and financially unaware, I suspect sharks looking to bite off chunks of that fortune for themselves rapidly surrounded him. But the root of the problem is that at the time he understood money only in terms of buying stuff.

I don't mean to pick on Mr. Tyson. (I'm not NUTS after all.) In this attitude towards money, he is not alone. The world is filled with athletes, performers, lawyers, doctors, business executives and the like who have been showered with money that all too often immediately flowed right off of them and into the pockets of others. In a sense, they never really had a chance. They never learned how to think about money.

It's not hard. Stop thinking about what your money can buy. Start thinking about what your money can earn. And then think about what the money it earns can earn. Once you begin to do this, you'll start to see that when you spend money, not only is that money gone forever, the money it might have earned is gone as well. And so on.

Clearly, none of this is to say we should never spend money. Rather, it is to fully understand the implications when we do. Consider buying a car for $20,000.

Even the least financially sophisticated person should see that once you buy the car you no longer have the twenty grand. I sure hope so, anyway.

However, distressingly it appears that most people don't understand that in choosing to lease or borrow money to buy their car they are basically saying, "Geez. I don't want to pay *twenty thousand dollars* for this car. I want to pay much, much more."

LEVEL II: CONSIDER OPPORTUNITY COSTS

What you might not have considered, and what I'd like you to look at now, is the concept that even if you pay in cash, that car is going to cost you far more than $20,000. There is an opportunity cost to no longer having that money available to work for you. "Opportunity cost" is simply what you give up when you commit your money to one thing (like a car) over another (like an investment), and it's easy to quantify.

All you need to do is select a proxy for how the money could be invested and earning for you should you choose not to spend it. Since I'll be constantly talking about (and explaining) VTSAX (Vanguard's Total Stock Market Index Fund) later in the book, let's use that.

For now, all you need to know is that VTSAX is a total stock market index fund and as such it mirrors the market's average returns of 8-12% annually. As our proxy it gives us a tangible number to use as our opportunity cost. Let's use the lower end of the range: 8%.

At 8%, $20,000 earns $1,600 per year. So your $20,000 car actually costs you $21,600. The original $20,000 plus the $1,600 it could have earned. But that's just in the first year, and you are suffering this opportunity cost every year. Over the 10 years you might own the car, that's 10 x $1,600: $16,000. Now your $20,000 car is up to $36,000.

That's really still understating things, however. We haven't even considered what those annual $1,600 chunks could have been earning themselves. And what those earnings could then have been earning. And so on.

Should you not already be depressed enough about all this, remember that the $20,000 is gone forever and so is the $1,600 in lost earnings year after year with no end. At the end of the day, it's one expensive damn car.

You have probably heard of "the magic of compounding." In short, the idea is that the money you save earns interest. That interest then earns interest itself. This causes a snowball effect as you earn interest on a bigger and bigger pool of money. Like the snowball it starts small, but as it rolls along it soon begins to grow in a rather spectacular fashion. It's a beautiful thing.

Think of opportunity cost as its evil twin.

One of the beauties of being financially independent is that by definition, you have enough money such that the power of compounding is greater than the opportunity cost of what you spend. Once you have your F-You Money, all you need do is make sure you continue to reinvest to outpace inflation and keep your spending below the level your stash can replenish.

If you are not yet financially independent and you see this as an attractive goal, you'll be well served to look at your spending through the prism of opportunity cost.

LEVEL III: HOW TO THINK ABOUT YOUR INVESTMENTS

Warren Buffett is rather famously quoted as saying:

- Rule #1: Never lose money.
- Rule #2: Never forget rule #1.

Unfortunately, too many people take this at face value and leap to the conclusion that Mr. Buffett has found a magical way to dance in and out of the market, avoiding the inevitable drops. This is not true and in fact he is on record speaking to the folly of trying: "The Dow started the last century at 66 and ended at 11,400. How could you lose money during a period like that? A lot of people did because they tried to dance in and out."

The truth is that during the crash of 2008-9, Buffett "lost" about 25 billion dollars, cutting his fortune from 62 billion to 37 billion. (That left over 37 billion being the reason I was wandering around at the time irritating friends by saying, "Gee. I only wish I could have lost 25 billion!")

Like the rest of us, Buffett was unable to time the market and in fact, knowing market timing to be a fool's errand, he didn't even try.

But unlike many others, Buffett didn't panic and sell. He knew that such events are to be expected. In fact, he continued to invest as the sharp decline offered new opportunities. When the market recovered, as it always does, so did his fortune. So did the fortunes of all who stayed the course. That's why I put "lost" in quotes.

Now there are likely many reasons Mr. Buffett didn't panic as that 25 billion dollars and all the potential it represented slipped away. Having 37 billion left surely helped. Though another clue is in how he thinks about the money in his investments.

Mr. Buffett talks in terms of owning the businesses in which he invests. Sometimes he owns them in part—as shares—and sometimes in their entirety. When the share price of one of his businesses drops, what he knows on a deep emotional level is that he still owns precisely the same amount of that company. As long as the company is sound, the fluctuations in its stock price are fairly inconsequential. They will rise and fall in the short term, but good companies earn real money along the way and in doing so their value rises relentlessly over time.

We can learn to think in this same way. Again, let's use VTSAX in exploring this idea.

Suppose yesterday you said, "Mmm. This idea of owning VTSAX makes sense to me. I'm gonna get me some." And having said that, you sent Vanguard a check for $10,000. At yesterday's close the price of VTSAX was $53.67. Your $10,000 bought you 186.3238308 shares.

If VTSAX shares are trading at $56 per share a week from now, you might say, "Mmm. My $10,000 is now worth $10,434. Yippee. Mr. Collins sure is smart."

If, however, the shares are trading at $52 per share a week from now, you might say, "Damn. My $10,000 is now only worth $9,689. That Collins guy is a bum."

That's the typical way average investors look at their holdings. As little slips of paper or, more accurately in this day and age, little bits of data that go up or down in value. If that's all they are, drops in the price on any given day can be very, very scary.

But there is a better, more accurate and more profitable way. Take a few moments to understand what you really own.

At $56 per share or at $52 per share, you still own the same 186.3238308 shares of VTSAX. That in turns means you own a piece of virtually every publicly traded company in the U.S.—roughly 3,700 the last time I checked.

Once you truly understand this, you'll begin to realize that in owning VTSAX you are tying your financial future to that same large, diverse group of companies based in the most powerful, wealthiest and most influential country on the planet. These companies are filled with hardworking people focused on prospering in the changing world around them and dealing with all the uncertainties it can create.

Some of these companies will fail, losing 100% of their value. Actually, they don't even have to fail and lose all of their value to fall off the index. Just dropping below a certain size or what's called "market cap" will be enough.

As those fall away, they are replaced by other newer and more vital firms. Some will succeed in a spectacular fashion, growing 200%, 300%, 1,000%, 10,000% or more. There is no upside limit. As some stars fade, new ones are always on the rise. This is what makes the index—and by extension VTSAX—what I like to call "self-cleansing."

If I were to seek absolute security (a very different thing than the smooth ride most mistake for safety), I'd hold 100% in VTSAX and spend only the ~2% dividend it throws off.

Nothing is ever completely certain, but I can't think of a surer bet than this.

We live in a complex world and the most useful and powerful tool for navigating it is money. It is essential to learn to use it. And that starts with learning how to think about it. It is never too late.

Oh, and somebody please send Mr. Tyson a copy of this book. It's not too late for him either.

Chapter 5

Investing in a raging bull (or bear) market

As of January 2015, the S&P 500 stood at 2,059, up sharply from its March 2009 low around 677. This is the very definition of a raging bull market. Whether you are considering investing a new chunk of cash that has come your way, or thinking about selling and sitting on the sidelines for a while, it is times like these that test your core investing principles and beliefs.

Here are some of mine:

- It is simply not possible to time the market, regardless of all the heavily credentialed gurus on CNBC and the like who claim they can.
- The market is the most powerful wealth-building tool of all time.
- The market always goes up and it is always a wild and rocky ride along the way.
- Since we can't predict these swings, we need to toughen up mentally and ride them out.
- I want my money working as hard as possible, as soon as possible.

For novice investors, it is very difficult not to look at the past market swings and think, "If only!" If only I had sold when it was up. If only I had bought when it was down. But wishing doesn't make this possible.

Since I launched www.jlcollinsnh.com in 2011, the market has been on one of its great bull runs, coming off one of its great bear crashes. On a fairly regular basis, I get questions and concerns like these:

- "Is NOW a good time to invest, right before a possible stock market crash?"
- "...a lot of people seem to think a stock market crash is just around the corner."
- "I fear I'm entering at the wrong time."
- "I'm afraid I'm investing right before a stock market crash..."
- "My fear had held me off for months, but I feel because I'm holding off I'm losing out."
- "I just want to get off to a good start, not a bad one."
- "Maybe I should wait until after the crash so I don't lose a chunk of money."
- "Should I just hold off until after a crash so I can make the most of my money?"
- "I'm just so fearful since I'm so new to this..."

If the market happened to be plunging into one of its periodic bear cycles these questions, and the psychology, would be much the same:

- "Should I wait until the market has bottomed out and then invest?"

This is all about fear and greed, the two major emotions that drive investors.

Fear is perfectly understandable. Nobody wants to lose money. But until you master it, such fear will be deadly to your wealth. It will prevent you from investing. Once you are invested, it will cause you to flee in panic for the exits every time the market drops. And drop—repeatedly on its relentless march upward—it will. The curse of fear is that it will drive you to panic and sell when you should be holding. The market is volatile. Crashes, pullbacks and corrections are all absolutely normal. None of them are the end of the world, and none are even the end of the market's relentless rise. *They are all, each and every one, expected parts of the process.*

Inevitably, as we'll discuss in Part II, there is a major market crash coming, and another after that. Over the decades you'll be investing, countless smaller corrections and pullbacks will occur as well. Learning to live with this reality is critical to successful investing over the long term. And successful investing is by definition long term. Any investing done short term is by definition speculation.

Therefore, if we know a crash is coming, why not wait to invest? Or, if currently invested why not sell, wait till the fall and then go back in? The answer is simply because we don't know when the crash will occur or end. Nobody does.

Don't believe me? Think you can? Test yourself here: http://qz.com/487013

You may have heard that a lot of people think a stock market crash is just around the corner. That's certainly true, but there are also lots of people who say we are just at the beginning of this boom and we will never see the S&P this low again. Every day, heavily credentialed experts are predicting a market crash. At the same time, equally credentialed experts are predicting a boom. Who's right? Beats me. Both are predicting the future and nobody can do that reliably.

So, why all the predictions? Simply because booms and busts are exciting! Get it right and your Wall Street/television reputation is made! Predicting them equals ratings, especially if the predictions are extreme. Predict the Dow soaring to 25,000 or crashing to 5,000 and people perk up. There is big money to be made doing this, for the gurus and cable TV shows anyway.

For serious investors, however, all of this is useless and distracting noise. Worse, if you pay attention to it, it is positively dangerous to your wealth. And your sanity.

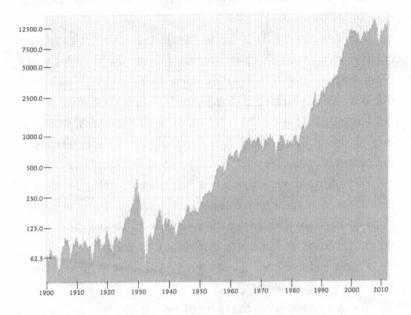

The Dow Jones Industrial Average 1900 – 2012
Graph adapted from www.stockcharts.com

History can help, but only on the broadest of scales. You see it in the chart above. The stock market always goes up. There are powerful reasons why. I can say—with almost absolute certainty—that 20 years from now the market will be higher than it is today.

I'd even say with a high degree of confidence that 10 years out it will also be higher. 120 years of market history bears this out.

However, this says nothing as to what the next few days, weeks, months or even years will bring.

Here's the problem. There is simply no way to know where in time we are.

Take another look at that chart. Could we be at a moment similar to January 2000 when the market peaked and went on to lose almost half of it's value? Or in July of 2007 when it did the same? Sure, it is easy to see that pattern in retrospect.

Or could that pattern have run its course, and now we find ourselves in a period more like the time the market passed 1,000 or 2,000 or 3,000 or 4,000 or 5,000? Where each level was left in the dust, never to be seen again? Beats me.

What we do know is that each of these milestones was surpassed at times like today when people were every bit as convinced that the market was too high and ready for a crash.

With that said, let's assume we do know that right now, at 2,102, the S&P 500 is at a peak and about to crash. Maybe a magic genie has told us so.

Clearly we'll sell (or at least not buy). But now what? We want the gains only the market can deliver. So we want back in at some point. But when? Is this a 10% pullback? If so, we'll want to buy at 1,892 or so.

What if it's a 20% decline, the official definition of a bear market? Then we don't want to buy until around 1,682.

But what if we do that and it turns out this is a crash!! Damn! In that case, we should have waited until it dropped all the way down to 1,200 or so. Where's that pesky genie when we *really* need him?

The point is that to play this market timing game well even once, you need to be right twice: First you need to call the high.

Then you need to call the low. And you must be able to do this repeatedly. The world is filled with sad investors who got the first right and then sat on the sidelines while the market recovered and marched right on past its old high.

Market timing is an un-winnable game over time. How can I be so sure? Simple:

The person who could reliably do this would be far richer than Warren Buffett, and twice as lionized.

Nothing, and I mean nothing, would be more profitable than this ability. That's what makes it so seductive. That's why gurus constantly claim they can do it, even if only a tiny bit. Nobody can. Not really. Not in any consistently useful way. Believing in Santa Claus is more profitable. Breeding unicorns is more likely.

But I don't care that this timing can't be done. Using the following illustration, let's demonstrate what I'd care about if I were you.

Let's assume you are 30 years old. You have some 60 or 70 investing years ahead. I'd look at that chart and note that some 60 years ago the Dow was trading at ~250. By January 2015 it was around 17,823. That's through 60 years of turmoil and financial disasters, just like the ones sure to come over the next 60 years.

Or just consider the last 20 years and the history of the S&P 500. In January 1995 it was around 500. By January 2015 it reached 2,059. And that includes 2000-2009, one of the all-time worst stretches in market history capped off by a crash second only to the Great Depression.

It is in this where the real magic is found. The stock market's wealth-building power over time is nothing short of breathtaking.

But so is the ride along the way. Whether you invest today or sometime in the future, I guarantee your wealth will be cut in half more than once over those 60 years. You'll suffer many other setbacks as well. It is never fun—but it is the process—and the price you and everybody else must pay to enjoy the benefits.

Thus the question is not "Should I invest in stocks now?" Rather it is "Should you invest in stocks at all?"

Until you can come to terms with the harsh facts above, the answer is no. Until you can be absolutely certain that you can watch your wealth get cut in half and still stay the course, the answer is no. Until you are comfortable with the risks that come with the rewards you seek, the answer is no.

In the end, only you can decide.

Fortunately, investing doesn't have to be an all or nothing proposition. If you are willing to give up some performance, there are ways to smooth out the ride a bit. It is done with asset allocation, which we'll discuss in Chapter 14.

Note:

In referencing the market's performance in this chapter, you may have noticed I jump between using the Dow and the S&P as the indexes. I prefer the S&P because it is broader and therefore a bit more precise. But the Dow goes back further in history and is more useful (and available) for the long view. If you overlay their charts over time, they track together with remarkable consistency, making them, for our purposes, indistinguishable.

PART II:

HOW TO HARNESS THE WORLD'S MOST POWERFUL WEALTH-BUILDING TOOL

"Simplicity is the keynote of all true elegance."

—Coco Chanel

CHAPTER 6

THERE'S A MAJOR MARKET CRASH COMING!!!! AND EVEN FAMOUS ECONOMISTS CAN'T SAVE YOU

One day a few years back, I found myself feeling a bit testy. I had just finished an article in a popular money magazine and reading this particular magazine is, in and of itself, enough to make me testy.

This particular article featured an interview with a famous economist and finance professor at an equally famous and prestigious university. There were impressive photos of the good professor looking serious and imposing.

To begin Part II of our financial journey together, I'm going to tell you some of what he said and why he's wrong. It is typical of the "common wisdom" you'll come across outside this book and in exploring it together we'll touch on some key subjects we'll examine in detail in later chapters.

Oh, and that major market crash that's coming? Don't worry. I'm also going to tell you why it doesn't matter.

First, in fairness to the famous economist, I have no quarrel with most of his ideas. Where I do, it is possible the good folks at the magazine didn't quite get it right. Perhaps they simply didn't place the emphasis correctly. Maybe someday this economist and I will have a few laughs over a cup of coffee about it. Or not.

In the interview the professor contends that the long-held theory of efficient markets—which says existing share prices almost instantly incorporate and reflect all relevant information—is morphing into what he calls the "adaptive markets hypothesis." The idea is that with new trading technologies the market has become faster moving and more volatile. That means greater risk. True enough and so far so good.

But he goes on to say this means "buy and hold investing doesn't work anymore." The magazine interviewer then points out, and good for him, that even during the "lost decade" of the 2000s, the buy and hold strategy of stock investing would have returned 4%.

The professor responds: "Think about how that person earned 4%. He lost 30%, saw a big bounce back, and so on, and the compound rate of return….was 4%. But most investors did not wait for the dust to settle. After the first 25% loss, they probably reduced their holdings, and only got part way back in after the market somewhat recovered. It's human behavior."

Hold the bloody phone! Correct premise, wrong conclusion. We'll come back to this in a moment.

Magazine: "So what choice do I have instead?"

Professor: "We're in an awkward period of our industry where we haven't developed good alternatives. Your best bet is to hold a variety of mutual funds that have relatively low fees and try to manage the volatility within a reasonable range. You should be diversified not just with stocks and bonds but across the entire spectrum of investment opportunities: stocks, bonds, currencies, commodities, and domestically and internationally."

Magazine: "Does the government have a role in preventing these crises?"

Professor: "It's not possible to prevent financial crises."

In the online comments for the article, a reader named Patrick nailed the flaw: "So, markets are efficient except when they're not. And buy and hold doesn't work because most people don't stick to it at the wrong time. OK wisdom, but is this news?" Gold star, Patrick.

Worse still is the professor's recommendation to hold "the entire spectrum of investment opportunities." This is his solution to dealing with the new investing world his "adaptive markets hypothesis" implies?

Seems odd, since he contends "buy and hold" no longer works, to suggest investors buy and hold nearly every asset class imaginable. Huh?

Let's accept the professor's premise that markets have gotten more volatile and will likely stay that way. I'm not sure I buy it, but OK, he's the credentialed economist. We can also agree that the typical investor is prone to panic and poor decision-making, especially when all the cable news gurus are lining up on window ledges. We certainly agree that it is not possible to prevent financial crises. More are headed our way.

So the question that matters most is: how do we best deal with it?

The professor (and many like him) says:

Treat the symptoms.

He defaults to the all too common canard of broad asset allocation. He would have us invest in everything and hope a couple of those puppies pull through. To do this properly would require a ton of work. You would need to understand all the various asset classes, decide what percentage to hold of each and choose how to own them. Once you did that you'd need to track them, rebalancing as necessary.

The result of all of this effort is to guarantee sub-par performance over time while offering the slim hope of increased security. I am reminded of the quote: "Those who would trade liberty for security deserve neither." I say:

Toughen up cupcake and cure your bad behavior.

This means you must recognize the counterproductive psychology that causes bad investment decisions—such as panic selling—and correct it in yourself. In doing so, your investments will be far simpler and your results far stronger.

To start you need to understand a few things about the stock market:

1. Market crashes are to be expected.
    What happened in 2008 was not something unheard of. It has happened before and it will happen again. And again. In the 40 odd years I've been investing we've had:

    *   The great recession of 1974-75.
    *   The massive inflation of the late 1970s and early 1980s. Raise your hand if you remember WIN buttons (Whip Inflation Now). Mortgage rates were pushing 20%. You could buy 10-year Treasury Notes paying 15% or more.
    *   The now infamous 1979 Business Week cover: "The Death of Equities" which, as it turned out, marked the coming of the greatest bull market of all time.

- The Crash of 1987, including Black Monday, the biggest one day drop in history. Brokers were literally on the window ledges and more than a couple took the leap.
- The recession of the early 1990s.
- The Tech Crash of the late 1990s.
- 9/11.
- And that little dust-up in 2008.

2. The market always recovers. Always. And, if someday it really doesn't, no investment will be safe and none of this financial stuff will matter anyway.

In 1974 the Dow closed at 616.*** At the end of 2014 it was 17,823.*** Over that 40 year period (January 1975 - January 2015) it grew, with dividends reinvested, at an annualized rate of 11.9%.* If you had invested $1,000 and just let it ride, it would have grown to $89,790** as 2015 dawned. An impressive result through all those disasters above.

All you would have had to do was toughen up and let it ride. Take a moment and let that sink in.

Everybody makes money when the market is rising. But what determines whether it will make you wealthy or leave you bleeding on the side of the road is what you do during the times it is collapsing.

3. The market always goes up. Always. Bet no one's told you that before. But it's true. Understand this is not to say it is a smooth ride. It's not. It is most often a wild and rocky road.

---

*   http://dqydj.net/sp-500-return-calculator/
     (Use: Dividends reinvested/ignore inflation)
**   http://dqydj.net/sp-500-dividend-reinvestment-and-periodic-invest-ment-calculator/
     (Click "Show Advanced" and check "Ignore Taxes" and "Ignore Fees")
*** http://www.mdleasing.com/djia-close.htm

But it always, and I mean always, goes up. Not every year. Not every month. Not every week and certainly not every day. But take a moment and look again at the chart of the stock market in the last chapter. The trend is relentlessly, through disaster after disaster, up.

4.   The market is the single best performing investment class over time, bar none.

5.   The next 10, 20, 30, 40, 50 years will have just as many collapses, recessions and disasters as in the past. Like the good Professor says, it's not possible to prevent them. Every time this happens your investments will take a hit. Every time it will be scary as hell. Every time all the smart guys will be screaming: Sell!! And every time only those few with enough nerve will stay the course and prosper.

6.   This is why you have to toughen up, learn to ignore the noise and ride out the storm; adding *still more* money to your investments as you go.

7.   To be strong enough to stay the course you need to know these bad things are coming—not only intellectually but on an emotional level as well. You need to know this deep in your gut. They will happen. They will hurt. But like blizzards in winter they should never be a surprise. And, unless you panic, they won't matter.

8.   There's a major market crash coming!! And there'll be another after that!! What wonderful buying opportunities they'll be.

I tell my 24-year-old that during her 60-70 odd years of being an investor, she can expect to see 2008 level financial meltdowns every 25 years or so. That's 2-3 of these economic "end of the world" events coming her, and your, way. Smaller collapses will occur even more often.

The thing is, they are never the end of the world. They are part of the process. So is all the panic that surrounds them. Don't worry. The world isn't going to end on our watch. It is hubris to think it will.

Of course, over those same years she's going to see several major bull markets as well. Some will rage beyond all reason, along with the hype that will surround them.

When those occur, the financial media will declare "this time it's different" with all the same confidence as when they claimed the end had come. In this too they will be wrong.

In the next few chapters, we'll discuss why the market always goes up, and I'll tell you exactly how to invest at each stage of your life, wind up rich and stay that way. You won't believe how simple it is. But yer gonna have to be tough.

Chapter 7

The market always goes up

In 1987, on what was later to be called Black Monday, I called my broker at the end of a very busy day. Remember that this was when we all still had stockbrokers. When we were in the dark ages before cell phones, personal computers, the internet and online trading.

"Hi Bob," I said cheerfully. "How's it going."

There was a long silent pause. "You're kidding," he said. "Right?" He sounded dreadful.

"Kidding about what?"

"Jim, we've just had the biggest meltdown in history. Customers have been screaming at me all day. It's a panic. The market is down over 500 points. Over 22%."

That was the point at which I joined the rest of the planet in being absolutely stunned. It is hard to describe just what this was like. Not even the Great Depression had seen a day like this one. Nor have we since. Truly, it looked like the end of the financial world.

A week or so later Time Magazine featured a cover with huge type declaring:

The Crash
After a Wild Week on Wall Street, the World is Different

Of course, in this they were completely wrong. Crashes, even huge ones like this, are a normal part of the process.

As any educated investor does, I knew that the market was volatile. I knew that on its relentless march upwards there could and would be sharp drops, corrections and bear markets. I knew that the best course was to hold firm and not panic. But this? This was a whole 'nother frame of reference.

I held tight for three or four months. Stocks continued to drift ever lower. I knew this was normal, but unfortunately I knew it only on an intellectual level. I hadn't yet learned it deep enough in my gut. Finally, I lost my nerve and sold.

I just wasn't tough enough. That day when I sold it was, if not the absolute bottom, close enough to it as not to matter. Then, of course and as always, the market again began its inevitable climb. The market always goes up.

It took a year or so for me to regain my nerve and get back in. By then it had passed its pre-Black Monday high. I had managed to lock in my losses and pay a premium for a seat back at the table. It was expensive. It was stupid. It was an embarrassing failure of nerve. I just wasn't tough enough.

But I am now. My mistake of '87 taught me exactly how to weather all the future storms that came rolling in, including the Class 5 financial hurricane of 2008. It taught me to be tough and ultimately it made me far more money than the admittedly expensive education cost.

As one of my blog readers put it: "We've stayed the course, with a side-dish of panic."

It's a great line, and staying the course is always served with a side dish of panic. That's why ya gotta be tough.

Here's our chart of the stock market's history again:

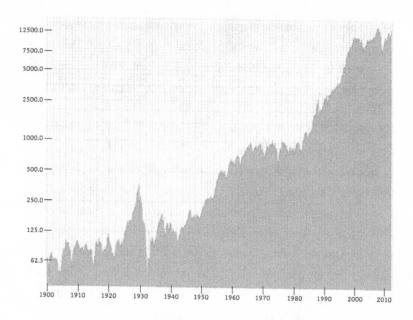

The Dow Jones Industrial Average 1900 – 2012
Graph adapted from www.stockcharts.com

Can you find my 1987 blip? It's there and easy to spot, but not quite so scary in context. Take a moment and let this chart sink in. You should notice three things:

1. Through disaster after disaster the market always makes its way higher over time.
2. It's a wild ride along the way.
3. There is a Big, Ugly Event.

Let's talk about the good news first. We'll tackle those other points later.

To understand why the market always goes up we need to look a bit more closely at what the market actually is.

Publicly traded companies are companies that issue stock that can be purchased by individuals and organizations. When you buy stock in a company you own a piece of that business. The stock market is made up of all the companies that are publicly traded.

The chart above represents the DJIA (Dow Jones Industrial Average). We are looking at the DJIA because it is the only group of stocks created as a proxy for the entire stock market going back this far. Way back in 1896 a guy named Charles Dow selected 12 stocks from leading American industries to create his Index. Today the DJIA is comprised of 30 large American companies.

But now let's shift away from the DJIA Index, which I only introduced for its long historical perspective, to a more useful and comprehensive index: the CRSP U.S. Total Market Index.

Don't let that technical sounding name scare you. For our purposes here, all you need to understand is that it is an index of virtually every publicly traded company in the U.S. More importantly, it is the index that Vanguard currently uses to model their Total Stock Market Index Fund, VTSAX. By design they are almost precisely the same. Since we can invest in VTSAX, going forward I'll be using it as our proxy for the stock market overall. Last time I checked, and this will vary, VTSAX held about 3,700 companies. This means that in owning VTSAX, you own a piece of all these businesses.

In 1976 John Bogle, the founder of The Vanguard Group, launched the world's first index fund. It tracked the S&P 500 index, allowing investors to own the largest 500 or so companies in the U.S. in one low-cost fund. It instantly became the single best tool for taking advantage of the market's relentless climb.

Then, in 1992, Vanguard created the Total Stock Market Index Fund and investors could own in this one fund not just the 500 largest U.S. companies, but virtually the entire U.S. stock market.

Now a quick note about something that can be confusing. Vanguard's Total Stock Market Index Fund comes in multiple varieties: VTSAX, VTSMX, VTI and a couple of others. We'll talk about why and how these vary a bit later. But what is important to understand now is that they each hold exactly the same portfolio created using that CRSP index. Essentially, they are the same. VTSAX is what's called the Admiral Shares version. It is the one I personally own and that's why I'm using it here.

So now we know what the stock market actually is and we can see from the chart that it always goes up. Let's take a moment to consider: how can this be? There are two basic reasons:

1. The market is self-cleansing.

Take a look at the 30 DJIA stocks. Care to guess how many of the original 12 are still in it? Just one. General Electric. In fact, most of today's 30 companies didn't exist when Mr. Dow originally crafted his list. Most of the originals have come and gone or morphed into something new. This is a key point: the market is not stagnant. Companies routinely fade away and are replaced with new blood.

The same is true of VTSAX. It holds almost every publicly traded company in the U.S. stock market. Now, picture all 3,700 of these companies along a classic bell curve graph that describes their annual stock performance.

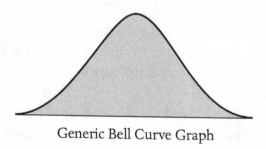

Generic Bell Curve Graph

Those few at the left will be the worst performing. Those few to the right, the best. All those between are at various points of performance.

What is the worst possible performance a bad stock can deliver? It can lose 100% of its value and have its stock price drop to zero. Then, of course, it disappears never to be heard from again.

Now let's consider the right side of the curve. What is the best performance a stock can deliver? 100% return? Certainly that's possible. But so is 200%, 300%, 1,000%, 10,000% or more. There is no upside limit. The net result is a powerful upward bias.

We could model all 3,700 stocks in VTSAX this way and we'd find that as some stars fade, new companies launch, grow, prosper and go public. This process of the new replacing the dead and dying is what makes the market (and VTSAX as its proxy) self-cleansing.

But note, this only works with broad-based index funds. Once "professional management" starts trying to beat the system, all bets are off. They can, and most often do, make things much worse and they always charge more fees to do so. We'll talk a bit more about this in a later chapter.

2. OWNING STOCK IS OWNING A PART OF LIVING, BREATHING, DYNAMIC COMPANIES, EACH STRIVING TO SUCCEED.

To appreciate why the stock market relentlessly rises requires an understanding of what we actually own with VTSAX. We own—quite literally—a piece of virtually every publicly traded company in the U.S.

Stocks are not just little slips of traded paper. When you own stock you own a piece of a business. These are companies filled with people working endlessly to expand and serve their customer base. They are competing in an unforgiving environment that rewards those who can make it happen and discards those who can't. It is this intense dynamic that makes stocks and the companies they represent the most powerful and successful investment class in history.

So, now we have this wonderful wealth-building tool that relentlessly marches upward but—and this is a major "but"—that causes many people to actually lose money in the market: boy howdy it's a wild and unsettling ride. Plus, there's that Big Ugly Event. We'll talk about those next.

Chapter 8

Why most people lose money in the market

In the preceding chapter, I presented to you a very rosy view of the stock market and its wealth-building potential. Everything I wrote is true. But, this too is true:

Most people lose money in the stock market.

Here's why:

1. We think we can time the market.

While stepping out when it is high and back in when it is low sounds enormously appealing, it is almost impossible to do. The reality is that we usually buy high and sell low, panicking when times are tough and buying when the market is soaring.

This applies to all of us. It is the way humans are hard-wired. Over the past twenty-odd years an array of academic papers have appeared investigating the psychology of investors. The results aren't pretty. Seems we are psychologically unsuited to prosper in a volatile market. The details of this research are beyond the scope of this book. But what is important is that it takes an act of will, awareness and effort to understand, accept and then change this destructive behavior.

Here's a sobering fact: The vast majority of investors in mutual funds actually manage to get worse returns from their funds than the funds themselves generate and report. Let that little nugget sink in for a moment. How can this be? Our psychology is such that we can't help trying to "time" the market. We tend to jump in and out, almost always at the wrong times.

2. WE BELIEVE WE CAN PICK INDIVIDUAL STOCKS.

You can't pick winning stocks. Don't feel bad. I can't either. Nor can the overwhelming majority of professionals in the business. The fact that this ability is so rare is the key reason why the very few who apparently can are so famous.

Oh, sure. Occasionally we can and, oh my, what a heady feeling it is when it works. It is incredibly seductive. Picking a stock that soars is an intense and addictive high. The media is filled with "winning" strategies that feed on this delusion.

I am not immune from the attraction. Back in 2011 I thought I had spotted a trend and as it happened made 19% in four months on the five stocks I chose. (Sigh. I still have this addiction.) That's almost 60% annualized, while the market was flat for the year. That's spectacular, if I do say so myself. It is also impossible to do year after year. It's a great rush, but a very poor foundation upon which to try and build wealth.

Even slightly beating the index year after year is incredibly difficult. Only a handful of investors have been able to modestly beat it over time. Doing so makes them superstars. That's why Warren Buffett, Michael Price and Peter Lynch are household names. That's why I don't let my occasional win go to my head. That's why I let index funds do the heavy lifting in my portfolio.

3. WE BELIEVE WE CAN PICK WINNING MUTUAL FUND MANAGERS.

Actively Managed Stock Mutual Funds (funds run by professional managers, as opposed to Index Funds) are a huge and highly profitable business. Profitable for the companies that run them. For their investors, not so much.

So profitable that there are actually more mutual funds out there than stocks. According to the U.S. News and World Report,* as of 2013 there were about 4,600 equity (stock) mutual funds operating in the U.S. Recall there are only about 3,700 publicly traded stocks in the U.S. You read that correctly. Yeah, I'm amazed too.

The article goes on to say about 7% of funds fail *each year*. At that rate, more than half (2,374 of those 4,600) will fold during the next decade.

With so much money at stake, investment companies are forever launching new funds while burying the ones that flounder. The financial media is filled with stories of winning managers and funds, and lavishly profitable advertising from them. Past records are analyzed. Managers are interviewed. Companies like Morningstar are built around researching and ranking funds.

The fact is, few fund managers will beat the index over time. In 2013, Vanguard posted the results of their research on this. Starting in 1998 they looked at all of the 1,540 actively managed equity funds that existed at the time. Over the next 15 years only 55% of these funds survived and only 18% managed to both survive and outperform the index.

82% failed to outperform the unmanaged index. But 100% of them charged their clients high fees to try.

---

*   http://money.usnews.com/money/personal-finance/mutual-funds/
     articles/2013/06/10/are-there-too-many-mutual-funds

While we can clearly see those that succeeded now, there is no predicting which funds will be in that rarefied 18% going forward. Every fund prospectus carries this phrase: "Past results are not a guarantee of future performance." It is the most ignored sentence in the whole document. It is also the most accurate.

Other academic studies suggest that when looking at longer time periods, even an outperformance rate of 18% is wildly optimistic. In the February 2010 issue of The Journal of Finance, Professors Laurant Barras, Olivier Scaillet and Russ Wermers presented their study of 2,076 actively managed U.S. stock funds over the 30 years from 1976 to 2006. Their conclusion? Only 0.6% showed any skill at besting the index or, as the researchers put it, the result was "...statistically indistinguishable from zero."

They are not alone. Brad Barber of UC Davis and Terrance Odean of UC Berkeley found that only about 1% of active traders outperform the market and that *the more frequently they trade, the worse they do.*

With this terrible track record, you might be wondering how is it that so many fund companies run ads that claim most, if not all, of their funds have outperformed the market. With so much money at stake it is not surprising that they have their tricks. One is simply to selectively choose a time frame for measurement that happens to work in their favor. Another just takes advantage of all those dead and dying funds.

Mutual fund companies launch new funds all the time. Random chance is enough to predict a few will do well, at least for a while. Those that don't are quietly closed and the assets folded into something doing better. The bad fund disappears and the company can continue to claim its funds are all stars. Cute.

There's lots of money to be made with actively managed funds. Just not by the investors.

4. WE FOCUS ON THE FOAM.

Imagine you've been reading this book on a nice warm summer's afternoon. Richly deserving of a reward, you crack open a bottle of your favorite brew and pour it into a nice chilled glass.

If you've done this before you know that if you carefully pour it down the side you'll wind up with a glass filled mostly with beer and a small foam head. Pour it fast and down the center and you can easily have a glass with a little beer filled mostly with foam.

Imagine now someone else has poured it for you, out of sight, and into a dark mug you can't see through. You have no way of knowing how much is beer and how much is foam. That's the stock market.

See, the stock market is really two related but very different things:

- **It is the beer:** The actual operating businesses of which we can own a part.
- **It is the foam:** The traded pieces of paper that furiously rise and fall in price from moment-to-moment. This is the market of CNBC. This is the market of the daily stock market report. This is the market people are talking about when they liken Wall Street to Las Vegas. This is the market of the daily, weekly, monthly and yearly volatility that drives the average investor out the window and onto the ledge. This is the market that, if you are smart and want to build wealth over time, you will absolutely ignore.

When you look at the daily price of a given stock, it is very hard to know how much is foam. This is why a company can plummet in value one day, and soar the next. This is why CNBC routinely features experts, each impressively credentialed, confidently predicting where the market is going next—while consistently contradicting each other. It is all those traders competing to guess how much beer and how much foam is actually in the glass at any particular moment.

While this makes for great drama and television, for our purposes it is only the beer that matters. It is the beer that is the real operating money making underlying businesses, beneath all that foam and froth, that over time drives the market ever higher.

Understand too, that what the media wants from these commentators is drama. Nobody is going to sit glued to their TV while some rational person talks about long-term investing. But get somebody to promise the Dow is going to 20,000 by year's end or, better yet, is on the verge of careening into the abyss, and brother you've got ratings!

But it's all just so much foam, fluff and noise. It doesn't matter to us. We're in it for the beer!

Chapter 9

The Big Ugly Event

So far we've seen that the stock market is a wonderful wealth-building tool that moves relentlessly upward. Vanguard's Total Stock Market Index Fund, VTSAX, is the only tool we need to access it.

But we've also seen that it is extremely volatile, crashes routinely and most people lose money due to their psychological tendencies. Still, if we toughen up, ride out the turbulence and show a little humility regarding our investing acumen, this is the surest path to riches.

Except......

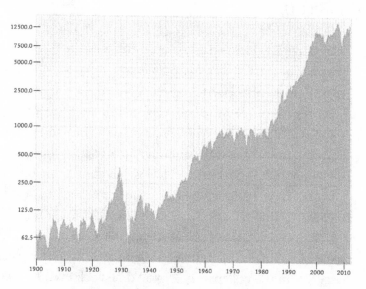

The Dow Jones Industrial Average 1900 – 2012

Graph adapted from www.stockcharts.com

There, in 1929, is the Big Ugly Event. The Mother of all Stock Market Crashes and the beginning of the Great Depression. Over a two year period, stocks plunged from 391 to 41, losing 90% of their value along the way. Should you have been unlucky enough to have invested at the peak, your portfolio wouldn't have fully recovered until the mid-1950s, 26 years later. Yikes. That's enough to try the toughest investor.

If you had been buying stocks on margin (that is, with money borrowed from your broker) as was all too common at the time, you would have been completely wiped out. Many speculators were. Fortunes were lost overnight. Never buy stocks on margin.

So what to do? Does the possibility of another Big Ugly Event blow a big enough hole in this idea of "toughen up and ride out the storms" to make it useless? The answer to that has everything to do with your tolerance for risk and your desire to build wealth. There are ways to mitigate the risk and we'll talk about them later.

For now, let's step back and consider a few key points regarding The Big Ugly:

1. It would have taken an investor of exceptionally bad luck to have borne the full weight of the crash. You would have had to buy your entire portfolio precisely at the 1929 peak.

    Suppose instead you had invested in 1926-27. Looking at our chart this is about halfway up on the climb to the peak. Many, many people were entering the market in these years. Certainly they were destined to lose all their gains, and yet 10 years later, had they held on, they'd be back in positive territory. Although another rough stretch was coming.

    Suppose you'd bought at the earlier peak in 1920. You would have taken an immediate hit and recovered five years later. From the collapse in '29 you'd be back even by 1936. Seven years.

The point is that any given start would have yielded a different outcome and one not as severe as the widely quoted 90% loss, peak to bottom.

2. Suppose you were just out of school and beginning your career in 1929. Assuming you were in the fortunate 75% that kept their jobs, you would have had decades of opportunities to buy stocks at bargain prices. Ironically, a crash at the beginning of your investing life is a gift. In fact, any pullback in stock prices is a gift while you are in the process of accumulating your wealth. It allows you to buy more shares for your dollars, on sale if you will.

3. Suppose in 1929 you were retired with a million dollars. By 1932 your portfolio is down 90%, to $100,000. A terrible hit for sure. But remember, the Depression was a deflationary event. That means the prices of goods and services fell dramatically, along with those of stocks. And that means your $100,000, while no longer a million, now had far more buying power than that same amount did pre-crash. Plus, it was poised to grow rather sharply from this low.

4. The Big Ugly Event has happened only once in the last 115 years. Longer actually, but that's how far back our DJIA data goes. We haven't had another in 86 years. Some even argue that with the controls put in place since 1929 it is unlikely we ever will again. While we can't be sure of that, we do know these are extremely rare events.

5. In 2008 we came right to the edge of the abyss. Closer I think than most folks fully appreciate. But we didn't tumble over. This I find encouraging.

What is not so encouraging is that a deflationary depression like that of 1929 is only one of the two possible economic disasters that can destroy wealth on a major scale.

The other is Hyperinflation.

Here in the U.S., we haven't had to deal with this monster since the Revolutionary War way back in 1776. But it destroyed Zimbabwe's economy as recently as 2008. Hungary had the worst case of it in history when in July 1946, the peak inflation rate reached 41.9 *quadrillion* percent, and many credit the German hyperinflation of the 1920s with ushering the Nazis to power in the 1930s.

Hyperinflation is very bad news—every bit as destructive as deflation—and it is exactly what it sounds like: Inflation running out of control.

A little inflation can be a very healthy thing for an economy. It allows for prices and wages to expand. It keeps the economic wheels greased and running smoothly. It is the antidote to looming deflationary depressions.

In a deflationary environment, delayed buying decisions are rewarded. If you were considering a new house in 2009-13 you would have noticed that prices were dropping, along with mortgage interest rates. Recognizing you could get both for less later, you waited. If enough potential buyers joined you, demand would drop pulling prices and rates down further. Delay is rewarded and action is punished. Too much of this and the market slips into a deadly spiral of crashing prices.

But during periods of inflation, anything you want to buy will cost more tomorrow than today. You have an incentive to buy that house (or car or appliance or loaf of bread) today and beat the price increase. Delay is punished with higher prices later and action now is rewarded. Buyers become ever more motivated. Sellers become ever more reluctant. Too much of this and the market slips into a deadly spiral of increasingly worthless currency people are desperate to exchange for goods.

Governments love a little inflation. They can add money to the system, keep the economy humming and not have to raise taxes or cut spending to do it. In fact, it is sometimes called "the hidden tax" because it erodes the buying power of our currency. It also allows debtors, like the government, to pay back their creditors with "cheaper dollars."

The good news for our VTSAX wealth-building strategy (which we'll discuss in depth in the next few chapters) is that stocks are a pretty good inflation hedge. As we've discussed, in owning stocks we own businesses. These businesses have assets and create products. The value of those rise with inflation, providing a hedge against the falling value of the currency. This is especially true in times of low to moderate inflation.

The decision every investor must make is how much risk to accept in the wealth-building process. Looking at the past 100+ years, you have to ask yourself whether it makes sense to focus on the Big Ugly or to invest in the relentless rise that has dominated history.

None of this is to say that Big Ugly Events are not very scary and destructive things. But they are rare and in the context of our overriding approach (spend less than you earn—invest the surplus—avoid debt), they are survivable.

In the next few chapters we'll look at specific investments to build and protect your wealth. As I promised in Part I, you won't believe how simple it is.

Chapter 10

Keeping it simple: Considerations and tools

Simple is good. Simple is easier. Simple is more profitable.

That's a key mantra of this book and what I'm going to share with you in these next couple of chapters is the soul of simplicity. With it, you'll learn all you need to know to produce better investment results than at least 82% (per the Vanguard Study referenced in Chapter 8) of the professionals and active amateurs out there. It will take almost none of your time and you can focus on all the other things that make your life rich and beautiful.

How can this be? Isn't investing complicated? Don't I need professionals to guide me?

No and no.

Since the days of Babylon people have been coming up with investments, mostly to sell to other people. There is a strong financial incentive to make these investments complex and mysterious.

But the simple truth is this: the more complex an investment is, the less likely it is to be profitable. Index funds outperform actively managed funds in large part simply because actively managed funds require expensive active managers. Not only are they prone to making investing mistakes, their fees are a continual performance drag on the portfolio.

But they are very profitable for the companies that run them, and as such are heavily promoted. Of course, those profits and promotional costs arise from all those juicy fees that come directly out of your pocket.

Not only do you not need complex investments for success, they actually work against you. At best they are costly. At worst, they are a cesspool of swindlers. They are not worth your time. We can do better.

Here's all you are going to need: Three considerations and three tools.

THE THREE CONSIDERATIONS

You'll want to consider:

1. In what stage of your investing life are you? The Wealth Accumulation Stage or the Wealth Preservation Stage? Or perhaps a blend of the two?
2. What level of risk do you find acceptable?
3. Is your investment horizon long-term or short-term?

As you've surely noticed, these three are closely linked. Your level of risk will vary with your investment horizon. Both will tilt the direction of your investing stage. All three will be linked to your current employment and future plans. Only you can make these decisions, but let me offer a couple of guiding thoughts.

Safety is a bit of an illusion.

There is no risk-free investment. Once you begin to accumulate wealth, risk is a fact of life. You can't avoid it, you only get to choose what kind. Don't let anyone tell you differently. If you bury your cash in the backyard (or in an FDIC insured bank account at today's near zero interest rates) and dig it up 20 years from now, you'll still have the same amount of money. But even modest inflation levels will have drastically reduced its spending power. If you invest in stocks, you'll likely outpace inflation and build wealth but you'll have to endure a volatile ride.

Your stage is not necessarily linked to your age.

The Wealth Accumulation Stage comes while you are working, saving and adding money to your investments. The Wealth Preservation Stage comes once your earned income slows or ends. Your investments are then left to grow and/or are called upon to provide income for you.

You might be planning to retire early. You might be worried about your job. You might be taking a sabbatical. You might be accepting a lower paid position to follow a dream. You might be launching a new business. You might be returning to the workforce after several years of retirement. Your life stages may well shift several times over the course of your life. Your investment stage can easily shift with them.

F-You Money is critical.

If you don't yet have yours, I suggest you start building it now. It is never too late to start. Be persistent. Life is uncertain. The job you have and love today can disappear tomorrow. Remember that nothing money can buy is more important than your fiscal freedom. In this modern world of ours, no tool is more important.

Don't be too quick to think short term.

Most of us are, or should be, long-term investors. The typical investment advisor's rule of thumb is: Subtract your age from 100 (or more aggressively 120). The result is the percentage of your portfolio that should be in stocks. A 60-year-old should, by this calculation, have 40% (or 60%) in stocks and 60% (or 40%) in conservative, wealth preserving bonds. Nonsense.

Here's the problem. Even modest inflation destroys the value of bonds over time and bonds can't offer the compensating growth potential of stocks.

If you are just starting out at age 20 you are looking at perhaps 80 years of investing. Maybe even a century if life expectancies continue to expand. Even at 60 and in good health you could easily be looking at another 30 years. That's long term in my book.

Perhaps you have a younger spouse. Or maybe you want to leave some money to your kids, grandkids or to a charity. All will have their own long term horizons.

THE THREE TOOLS

Once you've sorted through your three considerations, you are ready to build your portfolio and you'll need only these three tools to do it. See, I promised this would be simple!

1. Stocks: VTSAX (Vanguard Total Stock Market Index Fund). Stocks provide the best returns over time and serve as our inflation hedge. This is our core wealth-building tool. (See Chapter 17 for variants of this same fund.)

2. Bonds: VBTLX (Vanguard Total Bond Market Index Fund). Bonds provide income, tend to smooth out the rough ride of stocks and serve as our deflation hedge.

3. Cash. Cash is good to have around to cover routine expenses and to meet emergencies. Cash is also king during times of deflation. The more prices drop, the more your cash can buy. But when prices rise (inflation), its value steadily erodes. In these days of low interest rates, idle cash doesn't have much earning potential. I suggest you keep as little as possible on hand, consistent with your needs and comfort level.

We used to keep ours in VMMXX (Vanguard Prime Money Market Fund). At the time interest rates were higher and money market funds typically offered better interest rates than bank savings accounts. But with interest rates currently at historic lows, money market funds pay close to zero percent. Bank interest rates are now slightly higher. Plus they come with FDIC insurance on accounts up to $250,000.

For these reasons, we now keep our cash in our local bank and in our online bank, which happens to be Ally. Should interest rates rise and money market funds again offer better rates, we'll switch back.

So that's it. Three simple tools. Two index mutual funds and a money market and/or bank account. A wealth-builder, an inflation hedge, a deflation hedge and cash for daily needs and emergencies. As promised, it's low cost, effective, diversified and simple.

You can fine-tune your allocation in each investment to meet your own personal considerations. Want a smoother ride? Willing to accept a lower long-term return and slower wealth accumulation? Just increase the percentage in VBTLX and/or cash. Want maximum growth potential? Hold more in VTSAX.

In the coming chapters, we'll talk about index funds and bonds. Then we'll explore a couple of specific strategies and portfolios to get you started, and take a look at how to select the asset allocation best suited to your needs and temperament.

Chapter 11

Index funds are really just for lazy people, right?

Ah, no. Index investing is for people who want the best possible results.

Over the past couple of years, some of my investing ideas have drawn comment from other writers. While honored, I've noticed that even those folks seeking to compliment me sometimes frame my position on Vanguard and index funds as sound advice, but only for average people who don't want to work very hard at investing. The idea being that with a little more effort and smarts in the selection of individual stocks and/or actively managed funds, more diligent folks can do better.

Rubbish!

Back in Chapter 7, I introduced you to Jack Bogle. For my money (pun intended), no one has done more for the individual investor than Mr. Bogle. From launching Vanguard and its unique structure that benefits shareholders to creating index funds; he is a Titan in the financial industry, an investing saint and a personal hero.

Now in his 80s, here's what he has to say about successfully besting the market: "I've been in this business 61 years and I can't do it. I've never met anybody who can do it. I've never met anybody who's met anybody who can do it."

Neither have I.

This reality is something he had recognized decades earlier working on his thesis as a student and his decades in the business only served to confirm it. Namely, buying all the stocks in the market index reliably and consistently outperforms professional management, especially when taking costs into consideration.

The basic concept of indexing is that, since the odds of selecting stocks that outperform are vanishingly small, better results will be achieved by buying every stock in a given index. This idea fundamentally challenged and threatened the rationale behind paying high fees to Wall Street professionals. Not surprisingly, the pushback was swift and harsh. Mr. Bogle was roundly ridiculed at the time and in some quarters still is.

But increasingly over the past 40 years since his launch of the first index fund, the validity of Bogle's idea has been repeatedly confirmed.

The harsh truth is, I can't pick winning individual stocks and you can't either. Nor can the vast majority who claim they can. It is extraordinarily difficult, expensive and a fool's errand. Having the humility to accept this will do wonders for your ability to accumulate wealth.

There is even a school of thought that suggests superstar investors—think Warren Buffett, Peter Lynch and Michael Price—are simply lucky. Even for a hard-core indexer like me, that is tough to wrap my head around. Yet the research suggests that only 1% of the very top-tier of money managers outperform, and on the rare occasion they do it is hard to distinguish skill from luck.

So if this is the case, why do so many still resist the idea of indexing? I think there is a lot of psychology behind it. These are a few of the reasons that occur to me:

1. It is a challenge for smart people to accept that they can't outperform an index that simply buys everything. It seems it should be so easy to spot the good companies and avoid the bad. It's not. This was my personal hang-up, and I wasted years and many thousands of dollars in the vain pursuit of outperformance.

    Consider that in the 1960s the U.S. government was seriously considering (it never happened) the forced breakup of General Motors. GM was deemed so dominant and powerful that no other car company could compete. This is the same GM that survives today only by the grace of a huge bailout by that same government. On the other hand, back in the 1990s the smart money was betting Apple might not survive. As of this writing it is the single largest U.S. company as measured by market capitalization. Today's stars are tomorrow's wrecks. Today's fallen are tomorrow's exciting turnarounds.

2. To buy the index is to accept the market's "average" return. People have trouble accepting the idea of themselves or anything in their life as average.

    But in this context the word "average" is mostly misunderstood. Rather than meaning index fund returns are at the midpoint, the word "average" here means the combined performance of the all the stocks in an index.

    Professional money managers are measured against how well they do against this return. As we've seen, in any given year most underperform their target index. Indeed, over periods of 15 to 30 years, the index will outperform 82% to 99% of actively managed funds.

    This means just buying a total stock market index fund like VTSAX guarantees you'll be in the top performance tier. Year after year. Not bad for accepting "average." I can live (and prosper) with that kind of average.

3. The financial media is filled with stories of individuals and professionals who have outperformed the index for a year or two or three. Or in the very rare case, like Buffett, over time. (I cringe at the often-touted suggestion to just do what Buffett does. As if!) It's exciting and, after all, the companies that employ them are often advertisers. Or prospective advertisers.

   But investing is a long-term game. You'll have no better luck picking and switching winning managers than winning stocks over the decades.

4. People underestimate the drag of costs to investing.

   Paying fund and/or advisor fees of 1-2 percent seems low, especially in a good year. But make no mistake, these annual fees are a devil's ball and chain on your wealth. As a point of reference, the average mutual fund ER (expense ratio: the fee funds charge investors) is ~1.25%. The ER for VTSAX is .05%. As Bogle says, performance comes and goes but expenses are always there, year after year. After year. Compounded over time the amount lost is breathtaking.

   Consider this: Once you begin living on the returns from your portfolio you'll be able to spend roughly 4% of your assets per year. (We'll explore this 4% concept in Part IV) If 1% of your money is going to management fees, that is a full 25% of your income.

5. People want quick results, excitement and bragging rights. They want the thrill of victory and to boast about their stock that tripled or their fund that beat the S&P 500. Letting an

index work its magic over the years isn't very exciting. It is only very profitable.

As for me, I seek my excitement elsewhere and let indexing do the heavy lifting of my wealth-building.

6. Finally—and perhaps most influential—there is a huge business dedicated to selling advice and brokering trades to people who can be persuaded to believe they can outperform. Money managers, mutual fund companies, financial advisers, stock analysts, newsletters, blogs, and brokers all want their hand in your pocket. Billions are at stake and the drumbeat marketing the idea of outperformance is relentless. In short: we are brainwashed.

Indexing threatens the huge fees money managers and their lot routinely collect. They thrive on enabling your belief in the vain quest for the alluring siren of outperformance. It is no wonder they disparage indexing at every turn.

Many years ago I had a martial arts instructor who was talking about effective street fighting. On the subject of high kicks he had this to say: "Before you decide to use kicking techniques on the street ask yourself this question: 'Am I Bruce Lee?' If the answer is 'no' keep your feet on the ground." Good advice when you're playing for keeps.

As cool and effective as kicks look in the movies, tournaments and in the dojo, on the street they are very high risk. Unless you are both very skilled and significantly more skilled than your opponent (something unknowable in street fighting or investing) they are likely to leave you exposed and vulnerable. *Even*, and this is critical, *if you've had success with them before.*

So too with investing. Before you start trying to pick individual stocks and/or fund managers ask yourself this simple question: "Am I Warren Buffett?" If the answer is "no," keep your feet firmly on the ground with indexing.

Let me take a moment to be absolutely clear. I don't favor indexing just because it is easier, although it is. Or because it is simpler, although it is that too. I favor it because it is more effective and more powerful in building wealth than the alternatives.

I'd happily put in more effort for more return. More effort for less return? Not so much.

Chapter 12

Bonds

So far we've spent a fair amount of time looking at the stock market—stocks and the index funds we'll use to invest in them. Makes sense. They will serve as our wealth-building tool and will most likely be the largest part of our holdings.

But at various times we'll be adding bonds to the mix to smooth the ride, add a bit of income and provide a deflation hedge. Let's take a closer look.

Bonds are, in a sense, the more steady and reliable cousins to stocks. Or so it seems. But as we'll see, bonds are not as risk-free as many believe.

The challenge is that the subject of bonds is a BIG topic. The details are endless and most are unlikely to be of interest to the readers of this book. Heck, they're not all that interesting to me. Yet, unless you are comfortable just taking my word for it, you might want to know just what these things are and why they've found their way into our portfolio.

But how much information is enough? Beats me. So here's what we'll do. In this chapter I'll talk about bonds in stages. Once you've read enough to be comfortable owning the things (or not) you can just stop reading. If you get to the chapter's end and you want more, entire volumes have been written on the subject that can take you further.

STAGE 1

Bonds are in our portfolio to provide a deflation hedge. Deflation is one of the two big macro risks to your money. Inflation is the other and we hedge against that with our stocks. You'll recall from earlier that deflation occurs when the price of goods spirals downward and inflation occurs when they soar. Yin and yang.

Bonds also tend to be less volatile than stocks and they serve to make our investment road a bit smoother.

Bonds pay interest, providing us with an income flow.

Sometimes the interest is tax free, for example:

1. Municipal Bond interest is exempt from federal income tax and the income tax of the state in which the bonds are issued.
2. U.S. Treasury Bonds are exempt from state and local taxes.

STAGE 2

So what are bonds anyway, and how do they differ from stocks?

In the simplest terms: When you buy stock *you are buying* a part ownership in a company. When you buy bonds *you are loaning* money to a company or government agency.

Since deflation occurs when the price of stuff falls, when the money you've lent is paid back, it has more purchasing power. Your money buys more stuff than when you lent it. This increase in value helps to offset the losses deflation will bring to your other assets.

In times of inflation prices rise and so money owed to you loses value. When you get paid back your cash buys less stuff. Then it is better to own assets, like stocks, that rise in value with inflation.

Stage 3

Since we own our bonds in VBTLX—Vanguard's Total Bond Index Fund—most of the risks in owning individual bonds go away. At last count, and this will vary a bit, the fund holds 7,843 bonds. All are investment grade (top quality) and none rated lower than Baa (see Stage 4). This reduces default risk. The fund holds bonds of widely differing maturity dates, mitigating the interest rate risk. The fund holds bonds across a broad range of terms, reducing inflation risk.

In the next stages we'll talk more about these risks, but what's important to understand at this point is this: If you are going to hold bonds, holding them in an index fund is the way to go. Very few individual investors opt to buy individual bonds, with U.S. treasuries being the main exception, along with bank CDs which act like bonds.

Stage 4

The two key elements of bonds are the interest rate and the term. The interest rate is simply what the bond issuer (the borrower) has agreed to pay the bond buyer (the lender—you, or by extension the fund you own). The term is simply the length of time the money is being lent. So, if you were to buy a $1,000 bond at a 10% interest rate* with a 10 year term from XYZ company, each year XYZ would pay you $100 in interest (10% of $1,000) for a total of $1,000 over the life of the bond ($100 a year x 10 years). If you hold the bond until the end of the 10-year term it reaches its maturity date and the bond issuer is obligated to pay back your original $1,000 investment. The only thing you have to worry about is the possibility of XYZ defaulting and not paying you back.

---

* Of course interest rates are nowhere near 10% these days and I am only using this to make the math simpler.

So default is the first risk associated with bonds. To help investors evaluate the risk in any company or government bond, various rating agencies evaluate their creditworthiness. They use a scale ranging from AAA on down to D, kinda like high school. The lower the rating, the higher the risk. The higher the risk, the harder it is to find people to buy your bonds. The harder it is to find people to buy your bonds, the more interest you have to pay to attract them. Investors expect to be paid more interest when they accept more risk.

So default risk is also the first factor determining how much interest your bond will pay you. As a buyer of bonds, the more risk you are willing to accept the higher the interest you'll receive.

STAGE 5

Interest rate risk is the second risk factor associated with bonds and it is tied to the term of the bond. This risk only comes into play if you decide to sell your bond before the maturity date at the end of its term. Here's why:

When you decide to sell your bond you must offer it to buyers on what is called the "secondary market." Using our example above these buyers might offer more than the $1,000 you paid, or less. It depends on how interest rates have changed since your purchase. If rates have gone up, the value of your bond will have gone down. If rates have gone down, the value of your bond will have gone up. Confusing, no? Look at it this way:

You decide to sell your bond from our example above. You paid $1,000 and are earning 10%/$100 per year. Now, let's say interest rates have risen to 15% and I have $1,000 to invest. Since I can buy a bond that will pay me $150 per year, clearly I'm not going to be willing to pay you $1,000 for your bond that only pays $100. Nobody would, and you'd be stuck. Fortunately, however, the secondary bond market (where bonds are traded after they have been originally issued) will calculate exactly what lower price your bond is worth based on the current 15% interest rate. You might not like the price, but at least you'll be able to sell.

But if interest rates drop, the roles reverse. If instead of 10% they fall to 5%, my $1,000 will only buy me a bond paying $50 per year. Since yours pays $100, clearly it is worth more than the $1,000 you paid. Again, should you wish to sell, the bond market will calculate exactly what your higher price will be.

When interest rates rise, bond prices fall. When interest rates fall, bond prices rise. In either case, if you hold a bond to the end of its term you will, barring default, get exactly what you paid for it.

Stage 6

As you've likely guessed, the length of the term of a bond is our third risk factor and it also helps determine the interest rate paid. The longer a bond's term, the more likely interest rates will change significantly before it matures, and that means greater risk. While each bond is priced individually, there are three bond term groupings: short, medium and long. For example, with U.S. Treasury Securities (the bonds our federal government issues) we have:

- Bills — Short-term bonds of 1-5 year terms.
- Notes — Mid-term bonds of 6-12 year terms.
- Bonds — Long-term bonds of 12+ year terms.

Generally speaking, short-term bonds pay less interest as they are seen as having less risk since your money is tied up for a shorter period of time. Accordingly, long-term bonds are seen as having higher risk and pay more.

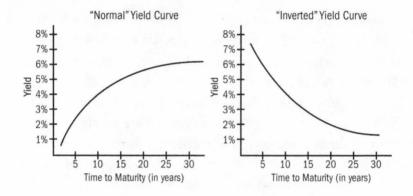

If you are a bond analyst, you'll graph this on a chart and create what is called a *yield curve*. The chart on the left is fairly typical. The greater the difference between short, mid and long-term rates, the steeper the curve. This difference varies and sometimes things get so wacky short-term rates become higher than long-term rates. The chart for this event produces the wonderfully named *Inverted Yield Curve* and it sets the hearts of bond analysts all aflutter. You can see what that looks like in the illustration on the right.

STAGE 7

Inflation is the biggest risk to your bonds. As we've discussed, inflation occurs when the cost of goods is rising. When you lend your money by buying bonds, during periods of inflation when you get it back it will buy less stuff. Your money is worth less. A big factor in determining the interest rate paid on a bond is the anticipated inflation rate. Since some inflation is almost always present in a healthy economy, long-term bonds are sure to be affected. That's a key reason they typically pay more interest. So, when we get an Inverted Yield Curve and short-term rates are higher than long-term rates, investors are anticipating low inflation or even deflation.

Here are a few other risks:

Credit downgrades. Remember those rating agencies we discussed above? Maybe you bought a bond from a company rated AAA. This is the risk that sometime after you buy the company gets in trouble and those agencies downgrade its rating. The value of your bond goes down with it.

Callable bonds. Some bonds are "callable," meaning that the bond issuer can pay them off before the maturity date. They give you your money back and stop paying interest. Of course they would only do this when interest rates are falling and they can borrow money more cheaply elsewhere. As you now know, when rates fall the value of your bond goes up. But if it gets called, poof! There goes your nice gain.

Liquidity risk. Some companies are just not all that popular and that goes for their bonds as well. Liquidity risk refers to the possibility that when you want to sell, few buyers will be interested. Few buyers = lower prices.

All of these risks are nicely mitigated simply by owning a broad-based bond index fund. That's why VBTLX is our choice.

STAGE 9

Municipal Bonds are bonds issued by governments and government agencies at the state and local levels. Typically these fund public works projects like schools, airports, sewer systems and the like.

While offering lower interest rates than corporate bonds, they have the advantage of being exempt from federal income taxes. They are also generally exempt from state income taxes for the state in which they are issued. This makes them appealing to folks in high income tax brackets, especially if they live in a high income tax state. It also makes them less expensive in interest payments for the governments that issue them.

Vanguard has several funds devoted to municipal bonds, including several focused on specific states. Anyone interested can check them out on www.vanguard.com.

Stage 10

There are precisely a gazillion different types of bonds. Basically they come from national governments, state and local governments, government agencies and companies. Term length, interest rates and payment terms are limited only by the imagination of the buyers, sellers and regulators. But since this is *The Simple Path to Wealth*, we can comfortably end this discussion here.

CHAPTER 13

PORTFOLIO IDEAS TO BUILD
AND KEEP YOUR WEALTH

We've spent these last few chapters getting to know the lay of the land, if you will. Now let's turn our attention to the fun stuff. How, exactly, can we use what we've learned so far to build and keep our wealth? I'm going to give you two portfolios, each using the tools (funds) we've discussed.

First I'll show you exactly what I tell my 24-year-old to do. She couldn't care less about investing, and with this simple approach she doesn't have to. All she needs to do is keep adding to the pot and let it ride. Years from now she'll wake up rich. Along the way she'll outperform over 82% of the more actively engaged investors out there. We'll call this The Wealth Accumulation Portfolio.

Then I'll share with you what my wife and I do as the semi-retired couple we are. We'll call that one The Wealth Preservation Portfolio.

Your personal situation is likely different from our family's. But using these two as parameters, and after reviewing your personal "considerations" as we discussed in Chapter 5, you should be able to fashion these tools into something that works for you.

This is what I've created for my daughter and what I tell her as to why.

Here's the thing: if you want to survive and prosper as an investor you have two choices. You can follow the typical advice we examined in Chapter 1 and seek out broad diversification with extensive asset allocations. Your hope is this will smooth the ride, even as it reduces your long-term returns.

Screw that! You're young, aggressive and here to build wealth. You're out to build your pot of F-You Money ASAP. You're going to focus on the best performing asset class in history: Stocks. You're going to "get your mind right," toughen up and learn to ride out the storms.

You've heard the expression, "Don't keep all your eggs in one basket."

You've likely also heard the variation, "Keep all your eggs in one basket and watch that basket very closely."

Forget it. Here's what your kindly old Uncle Jim says:

Put all your eggs in one basket and forget about it.

The great irony of investing is that the more you watch and fiddle with your holdings the less well you are likely to do. Fill your basket, add as much as you can along the way and ignore it the rest of the time. You'll likely wake up rich.

Here's the basket: VTSAX. No surprise here if you've been paying attention so far. This is the Total Stock Market Index Fund that holds virtually every publicly traded company in the U.S. That means you'll be owning a part of about 3,700 businesses across the country, making it a very big and diverse basket. The fact that it is a low-cost index fund keeps more of your money working for you.

Owning 100% stocks like this is considered a very aggressive investment allocation. It is aggressive and in this Wealth Accumulation Phase, you should be. You have decades ahead and you'll be adding new money as you go. Market ups and downs don't matter because you'll avoid panic and stay the course. If anything, you recognize drops as the "stocks on sale" buying opportunities they are. Perhaps 40 years from now (or whenever you are living on your portfolio) you might want to add a bond index fund to smooth the ride. Worry about that then.

At this point, I can see the financial gurus of the world gathering feathers and heating up the tar. So let me explain.

Previously, we explored the idea that financial crises are just part of the landscape and the best results come from simply riding them out. You can't predict them and you can't time them. Over your investing career you'll experience many of them. But if you are mentally tough enough you can simply ignore them.

So now if we agree that we can "get our minds right," what shall we choose for riding out the storm? Clearly we want the best performing asset class we can find. Just as clearly that's stocks. If you look at all asset classes from bonds to real estate to gold to farmland to art to racehorses to whatever, stocks provide the best performance over time. Nothing else even comes close.

Let's take a moment to review why this is true. Stocks are not just little slips of traded paper. When you own stock you own a piece of a business. Many of these have extensive international operations, allowing you to participate in all the markets across the globe.

These are companies filled with people working relentlessly to expand and serve their customer base. They are competing in an unforgiving environment that rewards those who can make it happen and discards those who can't. It is this intense dynamic that makes stocks and the companies they represent the most powerful and successful investment class in history.

Because VTSAX is an index fund, we don't even have to worry about which companies will succeed and which will fail. As we've seen, it is 'self-cleansing.' The failures fall away and the winners can grow endlessly.

A portfolio of 100% stocks—which is what VTSAX gives you—in study after study provides the greatest return over time. However if you are not tough enough to stay the course or if you get scared and bail when the storms are raging, you are going to drown. But that's a psychological failure, not a downside of this asset class.

As an aside, there are studies that indicate holding a 10-25% position in bonds with 75-90% stocks will actually very slightly outperform a position holding 100% stocks. It is also slightly less volatile. If you want to go that route and take on the slightly more complicated process of periodically rebalancing to maintain the allocation, you'll get no argument from me.

Could it really be this easy? Yep. I started investing in 1975. At the time VTSAX had yet to be created, but over the 40 years from January 1975 until January 2015, the S&P 500 index produced an annualized growth rate of 11.9%.* Just $2,400 a year ($200 per month) invested and left to ride would have grown to $1,515,542** by 2015. Over that same period, a one time lump sum investment of $10,000 would have become $897,905** This despite all the panics and collapses and recessions and disasters we've endured during these last 40 years.

---

*   http://dqydj.net/sp-500-return-calculator/
     (Use: Dividends reinvested/ignore inflation)
**   http://dqydj.net/sp-500-dividend-reinvestment-and-periodic-
     investment-calculator/
     (Click "Show Advanced" and check "Ignore Taxes" and "Ignore Fees")

Unfortunately, I wasn't smart enough at the time to do it. But this is *The Simple Path to Wealth* I created for my then 19-year-old daughter: Put all your eggs into one large and diverse basket, add more whenever you can and forget about it. The more you add the faster you'll get there. Job done.

THE WEALTH PRESERVATION PORTFOLIO

But wait you say, I'm at or nearing retirement. I've built my wealth. Now I want to hang on to it. Or maybe I'm just not comfortable with the volatility of an all or mostly stock portfolio. I want a smoother ride. What then?

Yeah, me too. A few years ago as I was nearing my own retirement I expanded beyond just VTSAX. Hold on now, this is going to get really complicated. You're going to have to add another index fund. Oh my!

We now enter the world of asset allocation and this will require slightly more of our time. In addition to adding the additional fund, we'll want to decide how much to allocate to each. Then once a year or so we'll want to rebalance to keep the allocations where we want them. It's going to take a couple of hours once a year. You can handle it.

As we know, a portfolio comprised of 100% stocks—even in the broadly diversified VTSAX—is considered very aggressive. High short-term risk (read: gut wrenching volatility) rewarded with top long-term results. Perfect for those who can handle the ride, are adding new money to their investments and who take the long view.

But it's not for everybody. Maybe you don't want to deal with this level of volatility. Maybe a bit more peace of mind is required. As you get older you might want to smooth the ride a bit, even at the cost of lower overall returns. You want to sleep at night.

Now that I'm kinda, sorta retired and we are financially independent, me too. My wife and I hold some other stuff in our portfolio. But not much. Here it is:

- **~75% Stocks:** VTSAX (Vanguard Total Stock Market Index Fund). Still our core holding for all the reasons we've discussed.
- **~20% Bonds:** VBTLX (Vanguard Total Bond Market Index Fund). Bonds provide some income, tend to smooth out the rough ride of stocks and are a deflation hedge.
- **~5% Cash:** We hold ours in our local bank.

You can fine-tune these allocations to your own personal considerations. Want a smoother ride? Willing to accept a potentially lower long-term return and slower wealth accumulation? Just increase the percentage in VBTLX. Comfortable with volatility? Want more growth? Add more to VTSAX.

Now that we've introduced this idea of asset allocation, we'll explore it a bit more next.

Chapter 14

Selecting your
asset allocation

Life is balance and choice. Add more of this, lose a little of that.
When it comes to investing, that balance and choice is informed
by your temperament and goals.

Financial geeks like me are the aberration. Sane people don't
want to be bothered. My daughter helped me understand this at
about the same time I was finally understanding that the most
effective investing is also the simplest.

Complex and expensive investments are not only unnecessary, they underperform. Fiddling with your investments almost
always leads to worse results. Making a few sound choices and
letting them run is the essence of success, and the soul of *The
Simple Path to Wealth*.

Reading this book so far you already know this. You also
know that, with simplicity as our guide, we look at our investing
lives in two broad stages using just two funds:

- The Wealth Accumulation Stage and the Wealth
  Preservation Stage. Or, perhaps, a blend of the two.
- VTSAX (Vanguard Total Stock Market Index Fund) and
  VBTLX (Vanguard Total Bond Market Index Fund).

The wealth accumulation stage is when you are working and have earned income to save and invest. For this stage I favor 100% stocks and VTSAX is the fund I prefer. If financial independence is your goal, your savings rate in these years should be high. As you invest that money each month it serves to smooth out the market's wild ride.

You enter the wealth preservation stage once you step away from your job and regular paychecks and begin living on income from your investments. At this point, I recommend adding bonds to the portfolio. Like the fresh cash you were investing while working, bonds help smooth the ride.

Of course, in the real world the divisions might not always be so clear. You might find yourself making some money in retirement. Or over the years you might move from one stage to the other and back again more than once. You might leave a high-paying job to work for less at something you love. In my own career there were many times I chose to step away from working for months or even years at a time. Each time changed my stage.

Using this framework of two stages and two funds, you have all the tools you need to find your own balance. In determining that balance you'll also want to consider two additional factors: How much effort you are willing to apply and your risk tolerance.

EFFORT

For the wealth accumulation stage an allocation of 100% stocks using VTSAX is the soul of simplicity. But as we've seen, some studies suggest that adding a small percentage of bonds—say 10-25%—actually outperforms 100% stocks. You can see this effect by playing with the various calculators found on the internet.

As you do, you'll notice that adding much beyond 25% bonds begins to hurt results.

Remember that these studies are not carved in stone and all calculators rely on making certain assumptions about the future. The difference in projected results between 100% stocks and an 80/20 mix of stocks and bonds is tiny. How those results actually unfold over the decades is likely to be equally close and the ultimate winner is basically unpredictable. For this reason, and favoring simplicity, I recommend 100% stocks using VTSAX.

That said, if you are willing to do a bit more work, you could slightly smooth out the wild ride and possibly outperform over time by adding 10-25% in bonds. If you do, about once a year you will want to rebalance your funds to maintain your chosen allocation. You might also want to rebalance any time the market makes a major move (20%+) up or down. This means you will sell shares in whichever asset class has performed better and buy shares in the one that has lagged.

Ideally you will do this in a tax-advantaged account like an IRA or 401(k) (we'll be talking about those shortly) so you don't have to pay tax on any capital gains. Having to pay capital gains taxes would be a major drawback and another reason to focus on holding just VTSAX. This rebalancing is simple and can be done online with Vanguard or most other investment firms. It should only take a couple of hours a year. But like changing the oil in your car, it is critical that you actually do it.

If you are unsure you'll remember to rebalance or simply don't want to be bothered, TRFs (Target Retirement Funds) are a fine option. These allow you to choose your allocation and then they will automatically rebalance for you. They cost a bit more than the simple index funds you'd use doing it yourself—you are paying for that extra service—but they are still low-cost. We'll discuss them in more detail in Chapter 16.

Risk Factors

Temperament. This is your personal ability to handle risk. Only you can decide and if ever there was a time to be brutally honest with yourself, this is it.

Flexibility. How willing and able are you to adjust your spending? Can you tighten your belt if needed? Are you willing to move to a less expensive part of the country? Of the world? Are you able to return to work? Create additional sources of income? The more rigid your lifestyle requirements, the less risk you can handle.

How much do you have? As we'll discuss in Part IV, the basic 4% rule is a good guideline in deciding how much income your assets can reasonably be expected to provide over time. If you need every penny of that just to make ends meet, your ability to handle risk drops. If, on the other hand, you are spending 4% but a big chunk of it goes towards optional hobbies like travel, you can handle more risk.

After considering effort and risk, here are some questions you'll want to consider.

When should I make the shift into bonds?

This is very much a function of your tolerance for risk and your personal situation.

For the smoothest transition, you might start slowly shifting into your bond allocation 5 or 10 years before you are fully retired. Especially if you have a fixed date firmly in mind.

But if you are flexible as to your retirement date and more risk tolerant, you might stay fully in stocks right up until you make the change. In doing so the stronger potential of stocks could get you there sooner. But if the market moves against you, you'll have to be willing to push your retirement date back a bit.

Of course, any time you shift between the accumulation and preservation stages, you'll want to reassess and possibly adjust your allocation.

Balance and choice. Yin and yang.

DOES AGE MATTER?

Overall, I prefer to divide our investment stages by life stages rather than using the more typical tool of age.

This is an acknowledgment of the fact that people are living longer and much more diverse lives these days. Especially the readers of this book. Some folks are retiring very early. Others are retiring from higher paid positions into lower paid work that more closely reflects their values and interests. Still others, like I did, are stepping in and out of work as it suits them, their stages fluidly shifting.

So age seems not to matter, at least not as much as it once did.

With that said, age does begin to limit your options as it advances. Age discrimination is a very real thing, especially in the corporate world. As you get older, you may not have all the same options readily available as you had in your youth. If your life journey involves stepping away from highly paid work occasionally, you'll do well to consider this.

Further, as you age you steadily have less time for the compounding growth of your investments to work and to recover from market plunges.

Both these considerations will influence your risk profile and you might well want to consider adding bonds a bit earlier if that's the case.

IS THERE AN OPTIMAL TIME OF YEAR TO REBALANCE?

Not really. I've yet to see any credible research indicating a particular time of year works best. Even if someone were to figure it out, once known everybody would rush to it, negating the effect.

I do suggest avoiding the very end/beginning of the year. It is a popular time for rebalancing and many are engaged in tax selling and new buying. I prefer to avoid the possible short-term market distortions this might cause. Personally, we rebalance once a year on my wife's birthday. Random and easy to remember.

I HAVE SOME OF MY INVESTMENTS IN TAX-ADVANTAGED ACCOUNTS AND SOME IN REGULAR ACCOUNTS. HOW CAN I REBALANCE ACROSS THOSE?

This can be cumbersome and you'll just have to work with what you have. While it is best to hold bonds in tax-advantaged accounts, it does complicate rebalancing.

First, you should be considering all your investments as a whole when figuring your allocation.

Next, as a rule it is better to buy and sell in tax-advantaged accounts to avoid creating taxable events. I recommend this unless you happen to have capital losses in a given year. Then it is best to take them in your taxable accounts when possible.

For instance, you might own VTSAX in both an IRA and in a taxable account. Should you need to sell to rebalance that year, sell in the taxable account to capture the loss. You can deduct it against any other gain you happen to have, including any capital gain distributions. You can also deduct up to $3,000 against your earned income. Any loss left over you can carry forward to use in future years.

(But be careful not to buy more VTSAX in your IRA, or any other of your investment accounts, within 30 days of selling. If you do, the IRS will consider this a "wash sale" and your tax loss would be negated.)

Does more frequent reallocation improve performance?

Investment firms that provide the service contend it can over time, but I'm not sure I buy the premise. If anything, my tilt is in the opposite direction. Which aligns me with Jack Bogle.

Mr. Bogle points to research Vanguard has done comparing stock and bond portfolios that were annually rebalanced and those not rebalanced at all. The results show the rebalanced portfolios outperformed but by a margin so slight it can be attributed to noise as much as the strategy. His conclusion:

"Rebalancing is a personal choice, not a choice that statistics can validate. There's certainly nothing the matter with doing it (although I don't do it myself), but also no reason to slavishly worry about small changes in the equity ratio."

We still rebalance annually, but were I to make a change it would be to not bother with it at all.

There you have it: The considerations you'll need to review and the tools you'll need to use to create the asset allocation that best fits your situation.

Now why in the world haven't I included international funds in the mix like most every other writer on investing? We'll look at that next.

Chapter 15

International funds

As we've discussed earlier in the book, most advisors recommend far more funds and asset classes than the two I've suggested. Indeed as we've seen—scared witless after the 2008-9 market implosion— many would now have us invest in everything in the hope a couple pull through. To do this properly would require a ton of work understanding the asset classes, deciding on percentages for each, choosing how to own them, rebalancing and tracking. All for what will likely be subpar performance.

Still, even for some who accept the advantages of simplicity, my two fund Wealth Preservation Portfolio seems incomplete. The readers of www.jlcollinsnh.com are an astute bunch and the missing asset class they ask about most frequently is international stocks.

Since almost every other allocation you come across will include an international component, why doesn't our Simple Path? There are three reasons: Added risk, added expense and we've got it covered.

1. Added Risk

Currency risk. When you own international companies they trade in the currency of their home country. Since those currencies fluctuate against the U.S. dollar, with international funds there is this additional dimension of risk.

Accounting risk. Few countries—especially in emerging markets—offer the transparent accounting standards required here in the U.S. Even here, companies like Enron occasionally cook their books and blow up on their investors. The weaker the regulatory structure in place, the greater the risk involved.

2. ADDED EXPENSE

VTSAX has a .05% expense ratio for rock bottom costs. While cheaper than comparable funds, even low cost Vanguard international funds have expense ratios at least twice that level.

3. WE'VE GOT IT COVERED

The key reasons cited for holding international funds are to avoid being dependent on the U.S. economy and to have exposure to the growth potential of world asset classes not correlated with the U.S. market. But we've got those covered.

Looking at the first, the 500 largest stocks in the U.S. make up about 80% of VTSAX. The largest of these 500 are all international businesses, many of which generate 50% or more of their sales and profits overseas. Companies like Apple, GE, Microsoft, Exxon/Mobil, Berkshire Hathaway, Caterpillar, Coca-Cola and Ford to name a few.

Since these companies provide solid access to the growth of world markets—while filtering out most of the additional risk—I don't feel the need to invest further in international-specific funds.

The second frequently cited reason is the expectation that the performance of international markets will not be correlated with that of the U.S. That is to say, when one is up the other might be down. The idea is having them as part of your asset allocation helps smooth the ride and offers the prospect of enhanced returns through reallocations. The problem is, as world economies become ever more closely knit together, this variation in the performance of their markets fades. While there will always be exceptions due to geopolitical events, world markets are becoming increasingly more correlated.

That's my take. Your worldview, however, may lead you to a different conclusion. If it does—and you feel the need for even more international exposure than that imbedded in VTSAX—our friends at Vanguard have some excellent options. Here are three I suggest:

- VFWAX: FTSE all-World ex-U.S. Index Fund (expense ratio .13%)
- VTIAX: Total International Stock Index Fund (expense ratio .12%)

Both of these invest everywhere in the world except the U.S., which you'll have covered with VTSAX.

If you prefer to keep things as simple as possible, at a bit higher cost, you might look at:

- VTWSX: Total World Stock Index Fund (expense ratio .25%)

This fund invests all over the world, including a roughly 50% allocation in the U.S. With it, you no longer even need to hold VTSAX.

While I don't feel the need for international funds, for those who do I don't strongly oppose holding them. Just be sure you understand what you already own in VTSAX and the cost in fees and additional risks these funds entail.

Chapter 16
TRFs: The simplest path to wealth of all

OK, you've read this far and while the Wealth Accumulation Portfolio requires only one fund and no effort, you need the Wealth Preservation Portfolio and that requires two. So you're thinking, "Aww man. Two funds? And I gotta rebalance them every year? That's too much to keep track of!" Maybe you are even thinking, "I get what he's saying in the last chapter, but I'd still like some international exposure in my portfolio."

I hear your pain. You need the simplest of all possible paths. You need to be able to buy just one fund and own it till your dying day. Any asset allocation crap should be handled for you. You have bridges to build, nations to run, great art to create, diseases to cure, businesses to build, beaches to sit on. I'm here for you bunkie.

More importantly, Vanguard is as well with a series of 12 TRFs (Target Retirement Funds). For that matter, so are other mutual fund companies, but as you know Vanguard is the primo choice around these parts so we'll be talking about their TRFs. If your 401(k) or similar plan offers only one of the others, what is said here (excepting expense ratio costs) still applies.

If you visit www.vanguard.com, you'll see that these 12 funds range from Target Retirement 2010 to Target Retirement 2060, plus one for those already in retirement at age 72 and above. The idea is that you simply pick the year you plan to retire and find the appropriate fund. Other than adding as much as you can to it over the years and arranging for withdrawal payments when the time comes, there is nothing else you need ever do. It's a beautiful and elegant solution.

Let's peek under the hood.

Each of these Target Retirement Funds is what is known as a "fund of funds." This just means that the fund holds several other funds, each with different investment objectives. In the case of Vanguard, the funds held are all low-cost index funds. As you know by now, that's a very good thing. The TRFs ranging from 2020 to 2060 each hold only four funds:

- Total Stock Market Index Fund
- Total Bond Market Index Fund
- Total International Stock Market Index Fund
- Total International Bond Market Index Fund

To those four funds the TR 2010, 2015 and 2020 funds add:

- Short-Term Inflation-Protected Securities Index Fund

As the years roll by and the retirement date chosen approaches, the funds will automatically adjust the balance held, becoming steadily more conservative and less volatile over time. You needn't do a thing.

The expense ratios range from .14% to .16%, depending on the fund. Not quite as low as a basic index fund like VTSAX (.05%), but very good considering the extra simplicity these offer.

What are the shortcomings?

Some people say the funds get too conservative too soon. Others complain that they are too aggressive for too long. For my money, I think Vanguard gets it pretty close to spot on. Maybe a bit conservative for me personally, but then I'm on the aggressive side. This is easy to adjust for. If you want a more conservative (greater percentage of bonds) approach, choose a date before your actual retirement. The earlier the date the more conservative the asset allocation. If you want more aggressive (greater percentage of stocks), just pick a later date.

Other fund companies use differing allocations for different retirement dates. If those are what's offered in your 401(k) or 403(b) plan, you'll need to take a look and decide accordingly. But the same principles apply.

Given these benefits and relatively low costs, I am comfortable recommending TRFs. They are an excellent choice for many, maybe even most people. They will certainly outperform the vast majority of active management investment strategies over time.

But I do have a slight preference for the approaches described in the earlier chapters. Here's why:

- The expense ratios are even lower than those of the TRFs.
- The TRFs all hold the Total International Stock Market Index Fund. While this is an excellent fund, as we discussed in Chapter 15 I don't feel the need for additional international coverage beyond that found in the Total Stock Market Index Fund, VTSAX.
- With separate funds, I can keep my bonds in my tax-advantaged bucket, protecting the dividends and interest from taxes. If you decide to own TRFs, they too are best held in a tax-advantaged bucket.

WHERE ARE YOU LIKELY
TO FIND TARGET RETIREMENT FUNDS?

Target Retirement Funds have become very popular as options in the 401(k) and 403(b) retirement plans offered by employers. The idea is most people really have very little interest in investing. Overall, this is sound thinking and TRFs provide an effective, simple and well-balanced "one decision" solution. Plus, because such retirement plans are tax-sheltered, the interest from the bonds and the dividends from the stocks go untaxed. Of course, other than those held in Roth 401(k) or Roth IRA accounts, when money is withdrawn in retirement taxes will be due.

WHAT SHOULD YOU DO?

If your company's retirement plan offers TRFs from Vanguard or low-cost equivalents from another fund company, they are well worth your consideration.

If you want a portfolio that's as simple as possible and still effective, TRFs are for you. They have *The Simple Path to Wealth* stamp of approval.

Chapter 17

What if you can't buy VTSAX? Or even Vanguard?

Throughout this book I've recommended two specific mutual funds:

- VTSAX (Vanguard Total Stock Market Index Fund)
- VBTLX (Vanguard Total Bond Market Index Fund)

These are the funds I own myself. In each case they are the "Admiral Shares" version of those portfolios. As such they have rock bottom expense ratios, but also require a minimum investment of $10,000.

While these "Admiral Shares" versions best fit my needs, they might not fit yours. Perhaps you are just starting out and the $10,000 minimum is still too steep. Or maybe they are not offered in your 401(k) plan.

Vanguard is also the only investment company I recommend or use, and we'll explore why in the following chapter. But maybe Vanguard itself is hard to access in the country where you live or in the 401(k) you are offered.

Not to worry. In this chapter we'll explore some alternatives.

Variations on the Funds

The first thing to understand is that VTSAX or VBTLX are each only one fund that holds the Total Stock Market Index and Total Bond Market Index portfolios, respectively. It is the portfolios that matter and Vanguard offers each in other flavors. For example, the exact same portfolio held by VTSAX can be found in six other funds, or what Vanguard calls "classes." Below I list them followed by their expense ratios and required minimum investment. The first three are for us individual investors:

- Admiral Shares: VTSAX .05% / $10,000
- Investor Shares: VTSMX .17% / $3,000
- ETF: VTI .05% (ETF=exchange traded fund)

You can buy ETFs in any amount you want, just like a stock. Note the expense ratio is just .05%, the same as that of the Admiral Shares. For this reason some people prefer to buy the ETF rather than the Investor Shares fund. Makes sense, but be careful. When buying or selling ETFs, just like a stock, commissions and/or spreads are frequently involved. These added costs can offset the savings in the expense ratio unless you have access to free trading.

These next three are "Institutional Shares" and you might find them in your 401(k) or other employer-sponsored retirement plan:

- VITPX: .02% / $200,000,000
- VITNX: .04% / $100,000,000
- VITSX: .04% / $5,000,000

So, when I recommend VTSAX you can substitute any of these if that's what is available and / or if one of the others better meets your needs. The important thing is that you are buying the Vanguard Total Stock Market Index portfolio.

Similar variations can be found for VBTLX and its Total Bond Market Index portfolio. If you visit www.vanguard.com and search for VBTLX, you'll find the home page for the fund. At the very top, under the fund name, you'll find links to the Investor and ETF versions.

When Vanguard isn't an option in your employer's tax-advantaged plan

Vanguard has a very active institutional business serving 401(k) programs and the like. But it very well may not be a part of yours. However, even if your tax-advantaged, employer-offered plan doesn't offer Vanguard you should still participate, certainly at least up to the amount needed to capture any employer match. Once you leave that employer you can easily roll your investments into an IRA with Vanguard.

So without Vanguard in your plan, the question becomes how to select the best option, which by now you know is a low-cost total stock and/or bond index fund.

The good news is that—due to the competitive pressure from Vanguard—nearly every other major mutual fund company now offers low-cost index funds. Just like the variations you can find in Vanguard of VTSAX, you can in all probability find a reasonable alternative in your 401(k). Here's what you are looking for:

1. A low-cost index fund.
2. For tax-advantaged funds you'll be holding for decades, I slightly prefer a total stock market index fund but an S&P 500 index fund is just fine.

3. You can also look for a total bond market index fund if your needs or preferences call for it. Most plans will also offer these.

4. TRFs (Target Retirement Funds) are frequently offered in 401(k) plans and these can be an excellent choice. But look closely at the fees. They are always higher than those for index funds, sometimes by a lot. For instance, the TRFs from Vanguard have expense ratios ranging from .14% to .16%, as compared to .05% for VTSAX. Those from other firms can run 5-6x higher.

FOR MY INTERNATIONAL READERS

If you live outside the U.S., Vanguard and its funds may or may not be available. Vanguard is growing rapidly and is now available in many countries outside the U.S. You can check out the list at: www.global.vanguard.com.

If Vanguard simply is not an option, in your fund search you'll want to follow the same guidelines as described above for tax-advantaged plans.

Also, when I talk about VTSAX or any Total Stock Market Index Fund, these are indexes that mirror the U.S. stock market. As I explained in Chapter 15, this is all those of us in the U.S. really need. But you might find it difficult to access such a U.S.-centric fund.

No worries. Take a look at a global fund like VTWSX (Vanguard Total World Stock Index). This is an index fund that invests all over the globe. In some ways I like it even better than my beloved VTSAX. I don't recommend it instead only because of its relatively steep expense ratio (.25%) and because VTSAX covers international pretty well for the reasons I describe in Chapter 15.

If you are inclined to go this route, you might consider the lower cost ETF version, VT (Vanguard Total World Stock ETF). Ordinarily, I tend to avoid ETFs (exchange traded funds) because of the possibility of sales commissions and/or spreads. But since the expense ratio on VT is .14% vs. .25%, it is worth exploring. Just be careful of the trading costs when you buy it.

One final caution. Be sure that whatever global fund you choose includes the U.S. market. It is a huge chunk of the world economy and you can't afford not to own a part of it. Many "international" funds—especially those offered by U.S.-based firms like Vanguard—are "ex-U.S. stocks," meaning they do not include U.S. based stocks. The reason is that they are designed to supplement the holdings of investors already in the U.S. market with VTSAX and the like. Makes sense, but likely doesn't suit your needs as an investor outside the U.S.

THE BOTTOM LINE

If I didn't have access to those two specific funds (VTSAX and VBTLX) or to the even lower expense ratio institutional versions, I'd look for the Vanguard variations that delivered the same Vanguard stock and bond index portfolios.

If I didn't have access to Vanguard, I'd look for similar low-cost funds from whatever sound investment company was available.

And if the future offered me the chance, I'd roll my holdings into Vanguard when I could.

CHAPTER 18

WHAT IS IT ABOUT
VANGUARD ANYWAY?

If you've read this far, you know I am a strong proponent of investing in Vanguard index funds. Indeed, unless you have no choice (as discussed in Chapter 17), my strong suggestion is that you deal only with Vanguard.

Understandably, such a bold recommendation is going to raise some questions. In this chapter we'll address the four most common:

1. WHAT MAKES VANGUARD SO SPECIAL?

When Jack Bogle founded Vanguard in 1975, he did so with a structure that remains unique in the investment world. Vanguard is client-owned and it is operated at-cost.

Sounds good, but what does it actually mean?

As an investor in Vanguard funds, your interest and that of Vanguard are precisely the same. The reason is simple. The Vanguard funds—and by extension the investors in those funds—are the owners of Vanguard.

By way of contrast, every other investment company has two masters to serve: The company owners and the investors in their funds. The needs of each are not always, or even commonly, aligned.

To understand the difference, let's look at how other investment companies (most companies, in fact) are structured. Basically, there are two options:

- They can be owned privately, as in a family business. Fidelity Investments is an example.
- They can be publicly traded and owned by shareholders. T. Rowe Price is an example.

In both cases the owners understandably expect a return on their investment. This return comes from the profits each company generates in operating its individual mutual funds. The profits are what's left over after the costs of operating the funds are accounted for—things like salaries, rent, supplies and the like.

Serving the shareholders in their mutual funds is simply a means to generate this revenue to pay the bills and create the profit that pays the owners. This revenue comes from the operating fees charged to shareholders in each of their individual funds.

When you own a mutual fund through Fidelity or T. Rowe Price or any investment company other than Vanguard, you are paying for both the operational costs of your fund and for a profit that goes to the owners of your fund company.

If I am an owner of Fidelity or T. Rowe Price, I want the fees, and resulting profits, to be as high as possible. If I am a shareholder in one of their funds, I want those fees to be as low as possible. Guess what? The fees are set as high as possible.

To be clear, there is nothing inherently wrong with this model. In fact it is the way most companies operate.

When you buy an iPhone, built into the price are all the costs of designing, manufacturing, shipping and retailing that phone to you, along with a profit for the shareholders of Apple. Apple sets the iPhone price as high as possible, consistent with costs, profit expectations and the goal of selling as many as they can make. It is the same with an investment company.

In this example I chose Fidelity and T. Rowe Price not to pick on them. Both are excellent operations with some fine mutual funds on offer. But because they must generate profit for their owners, both are at a distinct cost disadvantage to Vanguard. As are all other investment companies.

Bogle's brilliance, for us investors, was to shift the ownership of his new company to the mutual funds it operates. Since we investors own those funds, through our ownership of shares in them, we in effect own Vanguard.

With Vanguard, any profits generated by the fees we pay would find their way back into our pockets. Since this would be a somewhat silly and roundabout process and, more importantly, since it would potentially be a taxable event, Vanguard has been structured to operate "at cost." That is, with the goal of charging only the minimum fees needed to cover the costs of operating the funds.

What does this translate into in the real world?

Such fees are reported as "expense ratios." The average expense ratio at Vanguard is .18%. The industry average is 1.01%. Now this might not sound like much, but over time the difference is immense and it is one of the key reasons Vanguard enjoys a performance as well as a cost advantage.

With Vanguard, you own your mutual funds—and through them—Vanguard itself. Your interests and those of Vanguard are precisely the same. This is a rare and beautiful thing, unique in the world of investing.

2. Why are you comfortable holding all your assets with one company?

The answer is simple: It is because my assets are not invested in Vanguard. They are invested in the Vanguard mutual funds and, through those, invested in the individual stocks and bonds those funds hold. Even if Vanguard were to implode (a vanishingly small possibility), the underlying investments would remain unaffected. They are separate from Vanguard *the company*. As with all investments, these carry risk, but none of that risk is directly tied to Vanguard.

Now this can start to get very complex and for the very few of you who care, there's lots of further information you can easily Google. For our purposes here, what's important to know is the following:

You are not investing in Vanguard itself, you are investing in one or more of the mutual funds it manages.

- The Vanguard mutual funds are held as separate entities. Their assets are separate from Vanguard; each carrying their own fraud insurance bonds and their own respective board of directors charged with keeping an eye on things. In a very real sense, each is a separate company operated independently but under the umbrella of Vanguard.
- No one at Vanguard has access to your money and therefore no one at Vanguard can make off with it.
- Vanguard is regulated by the Securities and Exchange Commission (SEC).

All of this, by the way, is also true of other mutual fund investment companies, like Fidelity and T. Rowe Price. Those offered in your 401(k) are, in all likelihood, just fine too.

If you have an employer-sponsored retirement plan, like a 401(k), that doesn't offer Vanguard funds by all means invest in it anyway. As we'll discuss in Chapter 19, the tax deferral and any company match contributions make these plans attractive even with subpar fund choices and high fees.

3. WHAT IF VANGUARD GETS NUKED?

OK, let's be clear. If the world had ended on December 21, 2012 as the Mayan Calendar suggested it might, everything you had invested in Vanguard (or elsewhere) would have gone up in smoke. But, of course, that didn't happen.

If a giant meteor slams into Earth setting the world on fire followed by a nuclear winter, your investments are toast.

If space aliens arrive and enslave us all—unless you bought human feedlot futures—it's gonna mess up your portfolio.

But unlikely and beyond our control, not to mention the scope of this book.

That said, lesser disasters can and do happen. Vanguard is based in Malvern, Pennsylvania. What if, God forbid, Malvern is nuked in a terrorist attack? What about a cyber attack? Hurricane? Pandemic? Power outage?

Every major company and institution is aware of these dangers and each has created a Disaster Recovery Plan. Vanguard has one of the most comprehensive going. The company is spread across multiple locations. Its data is held in multiple and redundant systems. If you care to, you can check out their complete plan at www.vanguard.com.

However, if you are expecting a planet or even just a civilization-ending event, Vanguard's not for you. But then, no investments really are. You're already stocking your underground shelter with canned goods. Short of that, you can sleep just fine with your assets at Vanguard. I do.

4. AM I ON THE TAKE?

This book is such a strong proponent of Vanguard it is reasonable to ask: "Am I on the take?"

Nope. Vanguard doesn't know I'm writing this and they are not an advertiser on my blog. Nor do they pay me in any fashion whatsoever.

Chapter 19

The 401(k), 403(b), TSP, IRA and Roth buckets

So far, in Part II we've examined the market and looked at some sample portfolios built from the two key index funds I favor and TRFs. Those funds are what we call investments.

But in our complex world we must next consider where to hold these investments. That is, which investments go in which buckets? It is important to understand that 401(k)s, IRAs and the like are *not* investments themselves. Rather think of them as the buckets that hold the investments we choose. Broadly speaking, there are two types of buckets:

1. Ordinary Buckets
2. Tax-Advantaged Buckets

Now at this point I must apologize to my international readers. These next three chapters are about to become very U.S.-centric. I am completely ignorant of the tax situation and/or possible tax-advantaged buckets of other countries. My guess is that, at least for western-style democracies, there are many similarities. Most modern economies recognize the value of investing and seek to encourage it. Hopefully, it will be possible for you to extrapolate the information here into something relevant to where you live. If not, feel free to skip ahead.

Here in the U.S. the government taxes dividends, interest and capital gains. But it has also created several tax-advantaged buckets to encourage retirement savings. While well-intentioned, this has created a whole new level of complexity. Volumes have been written about each of these and the strategies now associated with them. Clearly, we haven't the time or space to review them all. But hopefully I can provide a simple explanation of each along with some considerations to ponder.

The Ordinary Bucket is where we hold investments that are not part of any tax-advantaged plan. It is, in a sense, no bucket at all. This is where everything would go were there no taxes on investment returns and no opportunities to defer them. We would just own what we own.

This is where we'll want to put investments that are already "tax-efficient." Tax-efficient investments are typically stocks and mutual funds that pay qualified dividends (dividends that receive favorable tax treatment) and avoid paying out taxable capital gains distributions. Such distributions are typical of actively managed funds that engage in frequent trading in their portfolios. VTSAX is a classic example of a tax-efficient investment. The dividends it pays are modest and mostly "qualified." Because trading (buying and selling) in the fund is rare, so too are taxable gains distributions.

Investments that are "tax-inefficient" are those that pay interest, non-qualified dividends and those that generate taxable capital gains distributions. These are things like some stock funds, bonds, CDs and REITs (real estate investment trusts). These we want to keep ideally in our tax-advantaged buckets as their payouts are then tax-deferred.

Let's look at our three investments and consider where they might fit:

- **Stocks**: VTSAX (Vanguard Total Stock Market Index Fund) currently pays around a 2% dividend and most of the gain we seek is in capital appreciation. It is tax-efficient and we can use our ordinary bucket. However, since this will be a large portion of our total holdings and since any investment can benefit from the tax-advantaged bucket, we will also hold it in our tax-advantaged buckets.
- **Bonds**: VBTLX (Vanguard Total Bond Market Index Fund): Bonds are all about interest payments. Other than tax-exempt municipal bonds, they go into our tax-advantaged bucket.
- **Cash**: is also all about interest but, more importantly, it is all about ready access for immediate needs. Ordinary Bucket.

None of this is carved in stone. There may be exceptions. Proper allocation should trump bucket choice. Your tax bracket, investment horizon and the like will color your personal decisions. But the above should give you a basic framework for considering the options.

Before we look at the specifics of IRAs and 401(k)s, this important note: None of these tax-advantaged buckets eliminates your tax obligation. They only defer it. Fix this in your brain. We are talking about when, not if, the tax due is paid.

When the time comes to withdraw this money, taxes will be due. So will penalties if you withdraw before age 59 1/2. And come age 70 1/2 (except for Roth IRAs) you will be required to begin withdrawals based on what the actuarial tables say your life expectancy will be. These are called RMDs, or Required Minimum Distributions. We'll discuss this in depth in the next chapter.

Don't let this scare you; simply be aware. The benefit of having your investments grow tax-sheltered over the decades is

no small thing and in most cases you should fund these buckets
to the maximum the law permits.

WITHDRAWAL STRATEGIES TO MINIMIZE TAXES

It is worth noting that there are strategies which seek to access this money tax-free, or at least at the lowest possible rate.
These involve structuring your earned and investment income
so as to fall under the limits the IRS establishes as being tax-
free. So while the money you withdraw is legally subject to tax,
your tax bracket is such that the actual amount owed is zero.

Staying under these limits can also provide the opportunity
to shift money tax-free over time from your Traditional IRA
to a Roth IRA (this is sometimes called a Roth Conversion
Ladder), thus further avoiding taxes when you withdraw and
spend it.

These are well worth considering if your situation allows
for them. You can find details in these posts:

From Go Curry Cracker:

- Never Pay Taxes Again: http://www.gocurrycracker.com/
  never-pay-taxes-again/
- GCC vs. The RMD: http://www.gocurrycracker.com/
  gcc-vs-rmd/

From The Mad Fientist:

- Early Retirement Strategies and Roth Conversion: http://
  jlcollinsnh.com/2013/12/05/stocks-part-xx-early-
  retirement-withdrawal-strategies-and-roth-conversion-
  ladders-from-a-mad-fientist/

- Traditional IRA vs. Roth IRA - The Final Battle: http://www.madfientist.com/traditional-ira-vs-roth-ira/
- Retire even earlier without earning more or spending less: http://www.madfientist.com/retire-even-earlier/

There are many variations of 401(k)-type and IRA-type accounts. We'll look at the basic types here. The rest are branches from these trees.

EMPLOYER-BASED TAX-ADVANTAGED BUCKETS

These are buckets provided by your employer, such as a 401(k). They select an investment company that then offers a selection of investments from which to choose. Many employers will match your contribution up to a certain amount. The amount you can contribute is capped. For 2016, the cap is $18,000 per person per year, or $24,000 for those age 50 and older. You can contribute to more than one plan (if you have access to more than one) but the cap is the total for all together, not for each separately.

In general:

- These are very good things, but not as good as they once were. Unfortunately many of the investment firms operating these programs have seized upon the opportunity to laden them with excessive fees. This is outrageous and offensive, but the advantage of having your investments grow tax free is not to be missed. Hold your nose and max out your contributions. I always did.
- Any employer match is an exceptionally good thing. This is free money. Contribute at least enough to capture the full match.

- Unless Vanguard happens to be the investment company your employer has chosen, you may not have access to Vanguard Funds. That's OK.
- Many 401(k) plans will have at least one index fund option. Scan the list of funds offered for the ones with the lowest ER (expense ratio). That's where you'll find the index funds, if any.
- When you leave your employer you can roll your 401(k) into an IRA, preserving its tax advantage. Some employers will also let you continue to hold your 401(k) in their plan. I've always rolled mine over. It gives you more control, greater investment choices and allows you to escape those ugly fees.
- You can contribute to both a 401(k) and a Roth 401(k), but the total must fall within the annual contribution caps.

401(k) and 403(b) Type Plans

- Contributions you make are deductible from your income for tax purposes.
- Taxes are due when you withdraw your money.
- Money withdrawn before age 59 1/2 is subject to penalty.
- After age 70 1/2 your money is subject to RMDs.

Roth 401(k)

- These are relatively new and not yet widely available. It is worth comparing these bullet points to those of the Roth IRA we'll discuss shortly.
- Contributions you make are NOT deductible from your income for tax purposes.

- All earnings on your investments are tax-free.
- All withdrawals after age 59 1/2 are tax-free.
- Once you reach age 70 ½ RMDs take effect.
- There is no income limit for participating.

TSPs (Thrift Savings Plans)

These are retirement plans for Federal employees, including military personnel. Think of them as a 401(k), but better.

Unlike the fee heavy cesspool too many 401(k) plans have become, a TSP offers a nice—but not overwhelming—selection of very low-cost index funds.

Looking at the government's chart of TSP expense ratios going back to 1999, these have ranged from a low of .015% in 2007 to a high of .102% in 2003. The reason for the variation, to quote the government website, is: "The TSP expense ratio represents the amount that participants' investment returns were reduced by TSP administrative expenses, net of forfeitures."

Even at their worst, these are very low expense ratios—often lower even than Vanguard index funds, and that's low! Good deal.

There are five basic TSP funds:

- The C-fund replicates the S&P 500 index.
- The S-fund replicates the small cap index.
- The F-fund is a bond index.
- The I-fund is an international stock index fund.
- The G-fund holds a non-marketable short-term U.S. Treasury security unique to TSPs.

Own both the C and the S in about a 75/25 balance and you've basically got VTSAX. But personally I wouldn't bother. I'd just hold the C-fund and be done with it.

In addition, there are the L-funds. These are "Lifecycle" funds made up of the other five held in various allocations designed for a particular time horizon. L-funds are very much like the Target Retirement Funds we discussed in Chapter 16.

TSPs are a no-brainer. If you are fortunate enough to have access to them, max them out. And in this one case, because of the ultra-low fees, I wouldn't roll them into an IRA once you leave your job.

INDIVIDUALLY-BASED TAX-ADVANTAGED BUCKETS: IRAS

IRAs are buckets you hold on your own in addition to and separate from any employer-sponsored 401(k)-type plans you may have. You have complete control in selecting the investment company and the investments for your IRA. This means you also control costs and can avoid those companies and investments that charge excessive fees. Mine are all with Vanguard.

You can only fund these with "earned income" or money you roll over from an employer-based plan. Typically, earned income is money you are paid for the work you do.

There are three types of IRAs. For 2016, the total contribution cap is $5,500 per year, or $6,500 for those age 50 and older. Note: This is in addition to the money you can contribute to your employer-based plan.

As with the 401(k) and Roth 401(k), you can contribute to both an IRA and a Roth IRA but again the total must fall within the IRA annual contribution caps.

Deductible and Roth IRAs both have income restrictions for participation. Non-deductible IRAs do not. These income limits change year to year and vary according to tax filing status and employer plan coverage.

Deductible IRA

- Contributions you make are deductible from your income for tax purposes.
- Deductibility is phased out over certain income levels.
- All earnings on your investments are tax deferred.
- Taxes are due when you withdraw your money.
- Money withdrawn before age 59 1/2 is subject to penalty.
- After age 70 1/2 your money is subject to RMDs.

Non-Deductible IRA

- Contributions you make are NOT deductible from your income for tax purposes.
- There are no income limits for participating.
- All earnings on your investments are tax-deferred.
- Taxes are due on any dividends, interest or capital gains earned when you withdraw your money.
- Taxes are not due on your original contributions. Since these contributions were made with "after tax" money they have already been taxed.
- Those last two points mean extra record keeping and complexity in figuring your tax due when the time comes.
- Money withdrawn before age 59 1/2 is subject to penalty.
- After 70 1/2 your money is subject to RMDs.

Roth IRA

- Contributions you make are NOT deductible from your income for tax purposes.
- Eligibility to contribute is phased out over certain income levels.

- All earnings on your investments grow tax-free.
- All withdrawals after age 59 1/2 are tax-free.
- You can withdraw your original contributions anytime, tax and penalty free.
- You can withdraw contributions that are conversions from regular IRAs after five years, tax and penalty free.
- You can withdraw as much as you like anytime to fund a first-time home purchase or to pay for college related expenses for yourself and/or your children.
- There is no RMD.

In short, these can be summarized like this:

- 401(k)/403(b)/TSP = Immediate tax benefits and tax-free growth. No income limit means the tax deduction for high income earners can be especially attractive. But taxes are due when the money is withdrawn.
- Roth 401(k) = No immediate tax benefit, tax-free growth and no taxes due on withdrawal.
- Deductible IRA = Immediate tax benefits and tax-free growth. But taxes are due when the money is withdrawn. Deductibility is phased out over certain income levels.
- Non-Deductible IRA = No immediate tax benefit, tax-free growth and added complexity. Taxes are due only on the account's earnings when the money is withdrawn. Contributions can be made regardless of income.
- Roth IRA = No immediate tax benefit, tax-free growth and no taxes due on withdrawal. A better Non-Deductible IRA, if you will. But eligibility phases out over certain income limits.

Now, if you've been paying attention, you might be thinking "Holy cow! This Roth IRA is looking like one very sweet deal. In fact it is even looking like it violates what Collins told us to fix in our minds earlier: "None of these eliminates your tax obligations. They only defer them." True enough, but as with many things in life there is a catch.

While the money you contribute to your Roth does indeed grow tax-free and remains tax-free on withdrawal, you have to contribute "after-tax" money. That is, money upon which you've already paid tax. This can be easy to overlook, but is a very real consideration.

Look at it this way. Suppose you want to fund your IRA this year with $5,000 and you are in the 25% tax bracket. To fully fund your deductible IRA all you need is $5,000 because, since it is deductible, you don't need any money to pay the taxes due on it.

But with a Roth, you'd need $6,250: $1,250 to pay the 25% tax due and still have $5,000 left to fund the Roth IRA. That $1,250 is now gone forever and so is all the money it could have earned for you compounding over the years.

Were you to fund your deductible IRA instead of your Roth, you'd still have this $1,250 which then could be invested in a taxable account. Of course, it is subject to your 25% tax bracket. After paying taxes on it, you'd have $937.50 left to invest ($1,250 x 0.75% = $937.50).

Curious as to what that might look like? Recalling that the average annual return on the S&P 500 for the 40 years from 1975-2015 was 11.9%*:

$937.50 invested each year
for 30 years @ 11.9%= $221,909**

---

*   http://dqydj.net/sp-500-return-calculator/
      (Use: Dividends reinvested/ignore inflation)
** http://www.calculator.net/investment-calculator.html
      (Click "End Amount" tab)

Of course, if you fail to invest the tax savings you'll lose this advantage and the Roth would have been the better choice.

It can be very emotionally satisfying to fund a Roth, pay the taxes now and be done with them. But it might not be the optimal financial strategy.

Because I'm the suspicious type, and the long-term tax advantages of a Roth are so attractive, I start thinking about what might go wrong. Especially since these are such long-term investments and the government can and does change the rules seemingly on a whim. Two potential threats occur to me:

1. The government could simply change the rules and declare money in Roth IRAs taxable. But this is doubtful. Roth IRAs have become so popular and are held by so many people, this seems more and more politically unlikely. Politicians are loathe to take anything away from voters.

2. More likely, the government could find an alternative way to tax the money. Increasingly in the U.S. there is talk of establishing a national sales tax or added value tax. While both may have merit—especially as a substitute for the income tax—these would effectively tax any Roth money as it was spent.

With all this in mind, here is my basic hierarchy for deploying investment money:

1. Fund 401(k)-type plans to the full employer match, if any.
2. Fully fund a Roth if your income is low enough that you are paying little or no income tax.
3. Once your income tax rate rises, fully fund a deductible IRA rather than the Roth.

4. Keep the Roth you started and just let it grow.
5. Finish funding the 401(k)-type plan to the max.
6. Consider funding a non-deductible IRA if your income is such that you cannot contribute to a deductible IRA or Roth IRA.
7. Fund your taxable account with any money left.

Let's finish this chapter with the recommendation that, whenever possible, you roll your 401(k)/403(b) (but not your TSP) accounts into your personal IRA. Usually this will be when you leave your employer. As we've already seen, employer plans are all too frequently laden with excessive fees and your investment choices are limited. In your IRA you have far more control.

Personally, I've always been slightly paranoid about having my employers involved in my investments any longer than I had to. The moment I could roll my 401(k) into my own IRA, I did.

One final note. We've touched a bit on tax laws in this chapter. While the numbers and information are current as of this writing, should you be reading this book a few years after publication, they are sure to have changed. The basic principles should hold up for some time, but look up the specific numbers that are applicable for the year in which you are reading.

CHAPTER 20

RMDs: THE UGLY SURPRISE AT THE END OF THE TAX-DEFERRED RAINBOW

Someday, if all goes well, you'll wake up to find you've reached the ripe old age of 70 1/2. Hopefully in good health, you'll rise from bed, stretch and greet the new day happy to be alive. You've worked hard, saved and invested, and now are contentedly wealthy and secure. Since you've diligently maxed out your tax-advantaged accounts, much of that wealth might well be in those, tax-deferred for all these years. On this day, if you haven't already, you'll begin to fully appreciate the "deferred" part of that phrase. Because your Uncle Sam is waiting for his cut and he figures he's waited long enough.

Except for the Roth IRA, all of the tax-advantaged buckets discussed in Chapter 19 have RMDs (required minimum distributions) as part of the deal and these begin at age 70 1/2. Basically this is the Feds saying "OK. We've been patient but now, pay us our money!" Fair enough. But for the readers of this book who are building wealth over the decades, there may well be a very large amount of money in these accounts when the time comes. Pulling it out in the required amounts on the government time schedule could easily push us into the very highest tax brackets.

Make no mistake, once you reach 70 1/2 these withdrawals from your IRAs, 401(k)s, 403(b)s and the like are no longer optional. Fail to take your full distribution and you'll be hit with a 50% penalty. Fail to withdraw enough and the government will take 50% of however much your shortfall is. That's right, *they will take half of your money*. This is not something you want to overlook.

The good news is that if you hold your accounts with a company like Vanguard, they will make setting up and taking these distributions easy and automatic, if not painless. They will calculate the correct amount and transfer it to your bank, money market, taxable fund or just about anyplace else you choose and on the schedule you choose. Just be sure to get the full RMD required each year out of the tax-advantaged account on time.

Just how bad a hit will this be? Well, there are any number of calculators online that allow you to plug in your exact numbers for an accurate read of your situation. Vanguard has their own, but so do companies like Fidelity and T. Rowe Price. To give you an idea of what the damage might look like, I plugged into Fidelity's to provide the following example.

You'll be asked your birth date, the amount of money in your account as of a certain date (12/31/13 when I did it) and to select an estimated rate of return. I chose January 1, 1945, $1,000,000 and 8%. No, those are not my real numbers. In a flash the calculator gave me the results year by year. Here's a sample:

Year	RMD	Age	Balance
2015	$39,416	70	$1,127,000
2020	$57,611	75	$1,367,000
2025	$82,836	80	$1,590,000
2030	$116,271	85	$1,742,000
2035	$154,719	90	$1,750,000

The good news is that even with these substantial withdrawals, the total value of our account will continue to grow. But, as we've discussed before, these are estimated projections. The market might do better or worse than 8% and it most certainly won't deliver 8% reliably each year on schedule.

The bad news is, not only do we have to pay tax on these withdrawals, the amounts could push us into a higher tax bracket. Or two. This, of course, will depend on how much income you have rolling in from your other investments, Social Security, pensions and the like.

To give you a frame of reference, here are the tax brackets for those married and filing jointly in 2016:

- 0 to $18,550   10%
- $18,551 to $75,300   15%
- $75,301 to $151,900   25%
- $151,901 to $231,450 28%
- $231,451 to $413,350 33%
- $413,351 to $466,950 35%
- $466,951 or more   39.6%

Based on this, we can see that even with no other income, by age 90 our taxpayer's RMD of $154,719 will put them in the 28% tax bracket even without considering any other income. And that's based on starting with only $1,000,000. Many readers applying the principles in this book starting in their 20s, 30s and 40s can easily expect to have several multiples of that by the time they reach 70 1/2.

Something that is important to note here—which confuses many people—is that this doesn't mean they pay 28% of the full $154,719 in taxes. Rather they pay 28% only on the amount over the $151,900 threshold of the bracket. The rest is taxed at the lower brackets on down. Should their other income bump them over the $231,450 threshold for the 33% bracket by, say, one dollar, they will only pay 33% in tax on that one dollar.

If you think of the RMD as the last money added, it is the money taxed at the highest rates. For instance, if they have $75,300 in other income, taking them right up to the 25% bracket line, any amount of RMD will be taxed at 25% or more.

All of this is before any other deductions and exemptions. Those serve to reduce your taxable income. While looking at all the possible variations is a discussion beyond the scope of this book, we can consider an example. For 2016 a married couple gets a standard deduction of $12,600 and personal exemptions of $8,100 ($4,050 each). In effect this means they don't reach the 25% bracket until their AGI (adjusted gross income) reaches $96,000. ($96,000 - $8,100 - $12,600 = $75,300)

So is there anything to be done? Possibly.

Assuming when you retire your tax bracket drops, you have a window of opportunity between that moment and age 70 1/2. Let's consider the example of a couple who retires at 60 years old, using the numbers above. They have a 10 year window until 70 1/2 to reduce their 401(k)/IRA holdings. They are married and filing jointly. For 2016:

- The 15% tax bracket is good up to $75,300.
- The personal exemption is $4,050 per person or $8,100 for our couple.
- The standard deduction is good for another $12,600.
- Add all this together and they can have up to $96,000 in income before they get pushed into the 25% bracket.

If their income is below $96,000, they might seriously consider moving the difference out of their IRA and/or 401(k) and taking the 15% tax hit. 15% is a low rate and worth locking in, especially given that 10 years from now their tax bracket could be twice that or more. It's true they lose the money they pay in taxes and what it could have earned—as we saw with the Roth vs. deductible IRA discussion in the last chapter—but we are now only talking about ten years instead of decades of lost growth. So, if they have $50,000 in taxable income they could withdraw $46,000 for a total of $96,000. They could put the $46,000 in their Roth, their ordinary bucket investments or just spend it. Rolling it into a Roth would be my suggestion and is in fact what I am personally doing.

You don't have to wait until you are 60 or even until you are fully retired to do this. Anytime you step away from paid work and your income drops, this is a strategy to consider. However, remember the further away from age 70 ½ you are, the more time you give up during which the money you pay in tax today could have been earning for you over the years.

There is no one solution. If as you approach age 70 ½ your 401(k)/IRA amounts are low, you can just leave them alone. If they are very high, however, starting to pull them out even at a 25% tax rate might make sense. The key is to be aware of this looming required minimum distribution hit so that, as much as possible, you can take it on your own terms.

Once again, in this chapter we've touched a bit on tax laws and the information is current as of 2016. By the time you are reading this book the laws may well have changed. Be sure to look up the specific numbers that are applicable for the year in which you are reading.

CHAPTER 21

HSAs: More than just a way to pay your medical bills

Much has been changing in the world of healthcare here in the U.S. While the opinions on these changes vary widely, one thing I can say with some certainty is that the number of people having access to and choosing high-deductible health insurance plans is likely to increase. These plans basically allow you to "self-insure" for part of your health care costs in exchange for lower premiums.

In the past, most health insurance plans came with very low deductibles and paid for most every medical cost beyond them. Those were the good old days.

As medical costs have skyrocketed, so have the insurance premiums required to provide such comprehensive coverage. Now, by having the insured shoulder some of the risk, the high-deductible plans are able to offer insurance against catastrophic illness and injury at more affordable rates. In exchange, the insured is responsible for paying the first medical bills out of pocket each year, typically $5,000-$10,000. To make this a bit more affordable and attractive, HSAs (Health Savings Accounts) were created to help handle these out-of-pocket expenses.

Basically, these are like an IRA for your medical bills and, as we'll see, the way they've been constructed creates some very interesting opportunities.

With an HSA, as of 2016, you can set aside up to $3,350 for an individual and $6,750 for a family each year. If you are 55 or older, you can add another $1000 to each of those.

Like an IRA, you can fund this account with pre-tax money. Or, put another way, your contribution is tax-deductible. You can open an HSA regardless of your income or other tax-advantaged accounts to which you might also be contributing. Here are some key points:

- You must be covered with a high-deductible health insurance plan to have an HSA.
- Your contributions are tax deductible.
- If you use a payroll deduction plan through your employer, your contribution is also free of Social Security and Medicare taxes.
- You can withdraw the money to pay qualified medical expenses anytime, tax and penalty free.
- Any money you don't spend is carried forward to be used whenever you need it.
- Qualified medical expenses include dental and vision, things often not part of health care insurance plans these days.
- You can use your HSA to pay the health care costs of your spouse and dependents, even if they are not covered by your insurance plan.
- If you withdraw the money for reasons other than to pay for medical expenses, it is subject to tax and a 20% penalty…
- Unless you are age 65 or over, or if you become permanently disabled; in which case you'll owe only the tax due.
- When you die, your spouse will inherit your HSA and it will become his or hers with all the same benefits.

- For heirs other than spouses, it reverts to ordinary income and is taxed accordingly.

This is also a good moment to point out that, while HSAs are often confused with FSAs (Flexible Spending Accounts), they are not at all the same. The key difference is that with a FSA, any money you don't spend in the year you fund the account is forfeited. The money in your HSA, and anything it earns, remains yours until you use it.

What we have here is a very useful tool, and one well worth funding for those who have access to it. But as promised above and as might be said on a late-night TV infomercial…

"Wait, there's more!"

Some additional key points:

- You are not required to pay your medical bills with your HSA.
- If you choose you can pay your medical bills out-of-pocket and just let your HSA grow.
- As long as you save your medical receipts, you can withdraw money from your HSA tax and penalty free anytime to cover them. Even years later.
- Those who plan to use this money to pay current medical bills are best served (as with all money you plan to spend in the short term) keeping it in a FDIC insured savings account.
- But, you can choose to invest your HSA anywhere. Such as in index funds like VTSAX.
- Once you reach the age of 65, you can withdraw your HSA for any purpose penalty free, although you will owe taxes on the withdrawal unless you use it for medical expenses.

As we sit back and ponder all this, an interesting option occurs. Suppose we fully funded our HSA and invested the money in low-cost index funds? Then we'd pay our actual medical expenses out-of-pocket, carefully saving our receipts, while letting the HSA grow and compound tax-free over the decades.

In effect, we'd have a Roth IRA in the sense that withdrawals are tax-free and a regular IRA in the sense that we get to deduct our contributions to it. The best of both worlds.

If we ever needed the money for medical expenses, it would still be there. But if not, it would grow tax-free to a potentially much larger amount. When we were ready, we would pull out our receipts and reimburse ourselves tax-free from our HSA, leaving any balance for future use. Should we be fortunate enough to remain healthy, after age 65 we would be able to take it out to spend as we please, just as with our IRA and 401(k) accounts, paying only the taxes then due.

And how about those nasty RMDs discussed in the last chapter? Well, so far the law has been silent on this point. It could go either way. Keep your fingers crossed.

The bottom line is that anyone using a high-deductible insurance plan should fund an HSA. The benefits are simply too good to ignore.

Once you do, if you choose you can turn it into an exceptionally powerful investment tool. I suggest you do.

CHAPTER 22

CASE STUDY: PUTTING
THE SIMPLE PATH TO WEALTH
INTO ACTION

So far we've discussed concepts and strategies to create your own simple path to wealth. For those few of you reading who are just starting out, this should be perfectly easy to implement. But most of you are already somewhere along your path. Perhaps you've made some mistakes and hold some investments you wish you had never made. Perhaps you hold too many different assets and realize now it doesn't have to be that complex. Regardless, you already have things in place that need to be considered. How, you might be asking, can I implement these ideas in the real world?

Clearly, I have no way of answering that for each reader who picks up this book. But in this chapter, I'll share with you a real-life reader case study drawn from www.jlcollinsnh.com.

For the purposes of this chapter, I've taken the liberty of consolidating this reader's questions and situation, and have done some editing for clarity. Other than that, where he is quoted all the words are his.

HIS NOTE:

"I'm 26 and have recently graduated from college, and decided to get my financial life in order. Luckily, I was able to find a great job and have no debt. I am working on saving up my emergency fund (roughly 24% of my income is going into it) and now I'm focusing my efforts on investments.

"My grandparents seeded an investment fund for all of their grandchildren when each was born. It has been managed by a financial advisor for years, and your posts have confirmed my thoughts that I can do better. It currently has around $35,000 in it in 12 different mutual funds.

"My grandmother doesn't remember the exact amount that started my account. Whenever a new grandchild was born, she would put in a starting amount equal to what was in the older children's accounts. The earliest record is from 1994. At the start of that year, there was approximately $6,700 in the account and $1,000 was added by my grandparents each year until it hit around $25,000. In 1994, the funds were half stocks and half bonds (my grandfather grew up during the Great Depression and didn't fully trust stocks).

"My employer offers a 403(b) plan and they match contributions up to 2.5%. Currently, I put 3% of my income into this. Vanguard's Total Stock Market Index Fund is one of the available options.

"I make $70,000 per year before taxes. Right now I'm saving 24% of my pay. My goal is to keep it at 20% or more, but realize I might have to drop to 15% if other commitments arise. I haven't really thought about when I want to retire. It would be great to retire early, but I have not officially set that goal.

"I think I'm also going to do a Roth IRA on my own.

"What is your suggestion on getting rid of my financial manager and all the mutual funds and buying into VTSAX? I don't fully understand the tax implications that are involved in that.

Correct me if I'm wrong, but $5,500 would go into the Roth and the rest into a traditional account. Is it okay to have the investments in my 403(b), Roth IRA, and my regular account in VTSAX?

"What is the best way to contribute to my funds? After I get my emergency fund built up and my money transferred to Vanguard, I will have around $1,000 per month. Do I put that in each month or wait to put in larger amounts. I have heard of dollar cost averaging, but haven't looked into it.

"Thanks for your advice and time."

THE BEGINNING OF MY RESPONSE WAS THIS:

"Before we get started, some congratulations are in order. No, not for you. For your grandparents!! They deserve big time major league kudos. Please tell them I said so.

"The fact that they have provided this seed capital for you and their other grandchildren tells me several things. They have resources, and that means they are fiscally responsible and effective in their own lives. They are generous. And, considering your questions and plans, clearly they have passed this on to their descendants. If you haven't already, take them out to dinner and raise a toast in their honor. If you already have, do it again."

LOOKING AT HIS SITUATION, WE HAVE A GREAT BASE UPON WHICH TO BUILD:

1. $35,000 in capital to start.
2. $70,000 salary and he is saving 24%, or $16,800 annually.
3. He wants to target saving about 20% going forward, or $14,000. As you'll see, I'll try to persuade him to increase that.

4. He's landed a good job with an employer that provides a 403(b) retirement plan.
5. Zero debt.
6. He's not sure about retirement yet—no surprise at age 26—but he recognizes the importance of F-You Money.
7. He wants to know how to contribute to his investments going forward and about dollar cost averaging.

Let's talk first about what investment to choose.

Fortunately, his employer's benefits plan offers Vanguard as an option. He is leaning toward Vanguard's Total Stock Market Index Fund and that idea is spot on. In fact, this is where we'll put all of his investments. He is in the wealth accumulation phase of his life and it's the right tool for the job.

In Chapter 17 we learned there are three options to owning this fund portfolio: Admiral Shares, Investor Shares and VTI, an ETF (Exchange Traded Fund). VTSAX is the Admiral version and provides the lowest cost, but has a $10,000 minimum buy-in. The Investor Shares option, VTSMX, holds the same portfolio, but with slightly higher costs and a $3,000 minimum. He should use Admiral Shares whenever he can and Investor Shares if needed as a start. Once the account reaches $10,000, Vanguard will automatically switch it to the lower-cost Admiral Shares.

As we've seen, this one fund gives him a portfolio that owns virtually every publicly traded company in the U.S. Since many of these have extensive international operations, he'll also have international market exposure. With this one investment he'll have broad diversification in the most powerful wealth-building asset of all: stocks. This allocation of 100% stocks is considered very aggressive and that's what we want for this phase. But be warned, as you know from reading the previous chapters, he can expect a wild and gut-wrenching ride. With that said, he's going to stick to the plan, keep investing and tough it out. At 26, he has decades ahead.

At some point he'll start thinking about retirement.

That retirement might not come until he's 65 or maybe he'll choose to implement it when he has F-You Money around age 35 or so. Whenever the time comes, as he approaches that phase he'll want to consider diversifying into bonds. But right now, in the wealth accumulation phase, stocks are where his money belongs and VTSAX is how best to own them.

Next let's look at the various investment buckets he has available and discuss how to allocate his VTSAX investment among them. You'll recall that these buckets are where we hold the investments we choose. In order of desirability the buckets are:

1. His 403(b) employer plan. Since he works for a university he has a 403(b) plan, rather than the 401(k) plans common in private industry. He plans to contribute 3% of his salary which will be tax deferred, and his employer matches 2.5%. That's free money! That makes this option #1.

2. Deductible IRA. This is very much like his employer plan in that his contributions to it are deductible and its earnings are tax-deferred. The important advantage, however, is that he has full control over his investment choice and is not limited to those in his plan. He will open his IRA with Vanguard and will choose VTSMX/VTSAX.

   Since his 403(b) options are excellent, this matters less in his case. But in many employer-based plans the choices available are not optimal. If you have such a plan, use the guidelines provided in Chapter 19 to find the option that most closely matches a total stock market index fund or an S&P 500 index fund. Most plans have versions of these. Fund it up to the maximum of any company match. Then turn to your personal IRA. Once that's fully funded, turn again to your employer plan up to the maximum.

Currently, the maximum annual IRA contribution limit is $5,500 and he should try to fund it as close to the limit as possible. The tax advantages are too sweet to leave behind.

3. Back to his 403(b). Current law allows him to contribute up to $18,000 each year to his 403(b) and at 3% he has only put in $2,100 so far. That leaves $15,900 in potential contributions.

Since he is only planning to save ~20%/$14,000 of his income he should contribute another $6,400 to his 403(b): $2,100 + $5,500 + $6,400 = $14,000. But as I said, we are going to try to persuade him to save more.

Instead he could max out his 403(b) plan by adding $15,900 to the $2,100 he is already contributing for the employer match, for a total of $18,000. Add to this the $5,500 going into his IRA and the total is $23,500. That's a saving rate of ~33.57%.

At this point it is worth noting that I am calculating these savings rates based on his pre-tax income. Some would argue that using post-tax income is better as that is what he actually has available to spend. But taxes are very complex and the post-tax income generated from any specific pre-tax income is likely to vary widely. Using pre-tax is just simpler and, because it tends to encourage saving greater dollar amounts, it is more in keeping with the ethic of this book.

For anyone serious about achieving financial independence, taking full advantage of all your tax-deferred opportunities is a must. And doing so starts to get you into a respectable saving rate. But there is no reason to stop here.

4. Ordinary Bucket. This is where we put regular investments made outside any tax-advantaged buckets. He'll pay taxes on the dividends and capital gains distributions each year but, unlike tax-advantaged accounts, the money is available anytime with no penalty. This is where his $35,000 spread across multiple mutual funds is now. When he moves it to VTSAX that will still be the case.

Once he sells the 12 funds he currently owns—assuming they have appreciated in value—he'll owe a capital gains tax. Given this relatively small amount of money and the fact that capital gains taxes are low at the moment, this is nothing to lose sleep over. However, were the amount significantly higher, this decision would become more complex. In such a case, it would require a thoughtful analysis of the investments currently held and their costs balanced against the tax liability.

So here is where we are: His savings rate is currently 24% as he builds an emergency fund, and he plans to reduce this to 20%. Compared to the average American these numbers are excellent. Compared to where he wants to be, he should consider doing more. A 50% savings rate is my suggestion, but others more committed to having F-You Money commonly reach for 70-80%.

He is already stepping out of the norm by being debt free, saving and investing. He is employed, young and childless. Never will he be in a stronger position to take it to the next level. At the very least, he should avoid "lifestyle inflation" by pledging that any salary increases will go towards his investments. If he does this now, in the future his problem will be how to spend all the money his money earns for him.

OK, with all that under our belt let's run some numbers and look at a couple of options, with their specifics.

We'll forget about reducing this to 20% as doing so doesn't get him where he wants to be.

He starts with the $35,000 from his grandparents and moves it immediately into VTSAX paying the capital gains tax, if any. As we've seen the average market return of the past 40 years (January 1975 - January 2015) has been ~11.9% annually.* At that rate his money doubles about every 6 years. By the time he is 62 (in 36 years) it will have doubled nearly 6 times over. A quick calculation shows he'll have over $2,000,000, *without adding a single penny*.** By the time he is 68 it will double again to ~$3,900,000. That's the power of compounding. Did I mention he should take his grandparents to dinner?

If you add to it as you go along, as he's going to, the results become even more dramatic. Using his current savings rate of 24% he'll have $16,800 of his $70,000 salary to invest each year.

His 403(b) gets 2.5% of his salary to capture the match, but he's contributing 3%. That's $2,100 per year (His employer will add 2.5%—another $1,750—but that's in addition to his 24%/$16,800 investment money). This will go into VTSAX as his plan offers it. If it did not, the money would go into the choice his plan offered that most closely resembles VTSAX.

His deductible IRA gets $5,500. That goes into VTSMX and this will move to VTSAX once over $10,000.

Between the 403(b) and the IRA we've accounted for $7,600 of his $16,800. For the remaining $9,200, we'll return to the 403(b) and put it there.

---

* http://dqydj.net/sp-500-return-calculator/
  (Use: Dividends reinvested/ignore inflation)
** http://www.calculator.net/investment-calculator.html
  (Click "End Amount" tab)

Don't let this three step process confuse you. It is only to walk through the selections in order of attractiveness. Once he's done that, the actual implementation would be simply:

1. Fund the 403(b) with $11,300 ($2,100 + $9,200)
2. Fund the IRA to the maximum of $5,500

OPTION #2: 50% SAVINGS RATE

Now let's see what happens if we can persuade him to get a little more serious about saving and investing. Again he starts with the $35,000 from his grandparents, but now we have another $35,000 (50% of $70,000) each year to invest from his salary.

As before his 403(b) plan gets 3% of his $70,000 salary—$2,100—and his employer matches 2.5%.

His deductible IRA investing in VTSMX also still gets the maximum contribution allowed, $5,500.

So between the 403(b) and the IRA we've again accounted for $7,600, but now leaving $27,400 to invest. With this we can take full advantage of the 403(b) by contributing $15,900 more. Add this to the $2,100 he contributed to get the match and he's reached the maximum annual limit of $18,000. And he still has $11,500 left over:

$$35,000 - \$2,100 - \$5,500 - \$15,900 = \$11,500$$

We'll add this $11,500 to VTSAX in the Ordinary Bucket and build on the $35,000 seed capital his grandparents so generously provided.

With option #2 it is not hard to see how much more powerfully his wealth will grow. He is taking full advantage of all the tax-advantaged plans available and is building wealth outside them that he can access anytime without penalty.

Of course, this requires that he organize his life in such a fashion as to live on the remaining $35,000. For some readers this might appear appallingly low; for others, extravagantly high. Either way it is certainly doable. It is simply a matter of choice and priorities and how much he values financial freedom.

Here's a fun fact: An income of $35,000 puts you in the top .81% of world incomes. Congratulations 1%'er! Want to know where your income puts you? Check it out here: www.global richlist.com

Finally, let's talk briefly about how these contributions will happen.

Like most people, he'll be investing as his money is earned. He'll be doing this with his 403(b), IRA and any additional money he adds to his ordinary bucket VTSAX account initially funded with the $35,000.

This is in effect a form of dollar cost averaging (DCA); that is investing chunks of money evenly over time. DCA is something we'll discuss in depth in Chapter 26.

The beauty of his 403(b) account is that once he sets it up, the contributions will happen automatically. The IRA and Ordinary Bucket VTSAX accounts will require him to expend a bit more effort. He'll either have to remember to add to them regularly—just like paying one's bills—or he can set them up with Vanguard to have the money automatically transfer. Automatic's what I'd do. It is easier and makes it more likely he'll stay the course.

There you have it. If he follows this simple path, he'll have F-You Money before he knows it and working will become optional. By the time he reaches his grandparents' age he will be well able to provide seed money accounts for his own grandkids, continuing the cycle. Around then he might also consider learning "How to give like a billionaire," which we'll discuss in Chapter 32.

Note:

If you are interested in the original version of this Case Study, you'll find it as a post titled **The Smoother Path to Wealth** on www.jlcollinsnh.com. You can find several more case studies there, each covering a different and unique situation. Just look under *Categories: Case Studies* in the right-hand column. For answers to a variety of simpler questions, click the button at the top labeled *Ask jlcollinsnh*.

Chapter 23

Why I don't like
investment advisors

Managing other people's money is a very big business, and for those who engage in it, a very lucrative one.

Since investing and managing money is highly intimidating for many folks, there is also an apparent need. This financial stuff just all seems so complex, it is not surprising that many people welcome the idea of turning it over to a professional who will, hopefully, get better results.

Unfortunately most advisors *don't* get better results. Investing only seems complex because the financial industry goes to great lengths to make it *seem* complex. Indeed, many investments are complex. But as you now already understand, not only are simple index investments easier, *they are more effective.*

Advisors are expensive at best and will rob you at worst. Google Bernie Madoff. If you choose to seek advice, seek it cautiously and never give up control. It's your money and no one will care for it better than you. But many will try hard to make it theirs. Don't let it happen.

When I say investment advisors, I am also referring to money managers, investment managers, brokers, insurance salespeople (who often masquerade as financial planners) and the like. Any and all who make their money managing yours.

Now, I'm sure there are many honest, diligent, hard-working advisors who selflessly put their clients' needs ahead of their own. Actually, I am not at all sure about that. But just in case, I put it out there in fairness to the few.

Here's the problem:

1. By design, structurally an advisor's interests and that of their clients are in opposition. There is far more money to be made selling complex fee-laden investments than there is in simple low-cost efficient ones. To do what's best for the client requires the advisor to do what is not best for himself. It takes a rare and saintly person to behave this way. Money management seems not the calling of the rare and saintly.

2. Well-intentioned but bad advice is endemic in this field. Advisors who put their clients' interests ahead of their own are, to steal a phrase from Joe Landsdale in his novel *Edge of Dark Water*, "rarer than baptized rattlesnakes." And then you've got to find one who is actually any good.

3. Advisors are drawn not to the best investments, but to those that pay the highest commissions and management fees. Indeed, often they are compelled by their firms to sell these types of investments. Such investments are, by definition, expensive to buy and own. And investments that are expensive to buy and own are, by definition, poor investments.

4. Not surprisingly, a field that provides access to people's life savings is a magnet for con men, thieves and grifters.

Let's take a look at how investment advisors earn their money, and how each method works against you. Remember now, here we are talking about those who are legitimate, rather than the outright crooks. Generally there are three ways:

1. COMMISSIONS

The advisor is paid each time you buy or sell an investment. These commissions in the investment world are called "loads."

It's not hard to see the potential for abuse here, and the conflict of interest is stark. There is no "load" (commission) charged to buy a Vanguard Fund. But American Funds, among others, charge a princely load. Typically it is around 5.75% and it goes directly into the pocket of the advisor. This means that if you have $10,000 to invest, only $9,425 actually goes to work for you. The other $575 is his. Mmmm. Wonder which he'll recommend?

Some funds offer a 1% recurring management fee to the advisors who sell them. That means you get to pay a commission not only once, but every year for as long as you hold the fund. No surprise advisors favor these too. Often this fee *and* a load are found in the same investment.

Further, since these funds are most often actively managed, they carry a high expense ratio and are mostly doomed to underperform the simple low-cost index funds we can so easily buy on our own.

Consider how all this can add up. Take a 5.75% load, combined with a 1% management fee, along with an expense ratio of, say, 1.5% and you've given up 8.25% of your capital right from the start. That's money you not only lose forever, you also lose all the money it could have earned for you over the decades. Compare that with the 0.05% expense ratio of VTSAX. Holy Crap!

Insurance investments are some of the highest commission payers. This makes them perhaps the most aggressively recommended products advisors offer and certainly among the most costly to you. Annuities and whole/universal life insurance carry commissions as high as 10%. Worse, these commissions are buried in the investment so you never see them. How such fraud is legal I can't say. But it is.

Hedge funds and private investments all make their salespeople wealthy, along with the operators. Investors? Maybe. Sometimes. Nah, not so much.

Remember Bernie Madoff? People literally *begged* him to take their money. His credentials were impeccable. His track record too. Only the "best" investment advisors could get you in. Mr. Madoff paid them handsomely to do so. As did their clients. Oops.

If all this weren't enough, if you're not paying attention, there is more money to be mined at your expense by "churning" your account. Churning refers to the frequent buying and selling of investments to generate commissions. It is illegal. But it is also easily disguised, principally as "adjusting your asset allocation."

2. The AUM (Assets Under Management) Model

With the rampant abuse of the commission model, in recent years charging flat management fees has grown in popularity. These fees are typically 1-2% of the client's total assets and this approach is presented as being more objective and "professional." But there are snakes in this grass as well.

First, 1-2% annually is a HUGE drag on the growth of your wealth and on your income once you are living off it. Investment returns are precious and under this model your advisor is skimming the absolute cream.

Suppose you have a nest egg of $100,000. That's about the minimum needed to interest an advisor. Let's further suppose you invest it for 20 years and earn 11.9% per year which as we've seen is the average annual return of the past 40 years (January 1975 - January 2015)*. You end up with $947,549.** Not bad. Now suppose you give up 2% of these annual gains to a management fee. Your net return is now 9.9% and after 20 years that yields $660,623.** That's a whopping *$286,926 less.* Yikes! You not only give up the 2% each year, you give up all the money that money would have earned compounding for you over the 20 year period. Let me hammer this point home—it's a very big deal.

Second, we still have the problem of a conflict of interest. With the AUM model it is not as pervasive as with the commission model, but it's still there. Maybe you are considering paying off your $100,000 mortgage. Or perhaps you're thinking about whether to contribute $100,000 to your kid's college education so they can avoid going into debt. Often advisors will advise against either of these courses. For you, depending on your situation, that may be good or bad advice. For your advisor, it is the only advice that preserves the $1,000 to $2,000 in annual fees that $100,000 puts in their pocket.

Third, the vast, vast majority of advisors are destined to cost you still more money as they underperform the market. The actively managed funds they tend to choose woefully underperform the index. You won't know for 20 years or so if you got lucky enough to pick one of the exceedingly rare ones that don't.

---

*   http://dqydj.net/sp-500-return-calculator/
     (Use: Dividends reinvested/ignore inflation)
**   http://www.calculator.net/investment-calculator.html
     (Click "End Amount" tab)

3. Hourly fees

Many advisors tend to dislike this model, pointing out that it often limits the time a client is willing to spend with them. That's true as far as it goes, but it is also true that it takes a lot of hours to equal the money that can be made in commissions and annual fees.

They also point out that clients are less likely to object to commissions and fees because they tend not to notice these being skimmed off the top. Paying an hourly rate—even when it is more cost effective—requires writing out the check and actually seeing the money leave your hands. That's uncomfortable for the clients and that means less money for the advisor. Not such a bad thing for the clients, seems to me.

That said, if you really need advice, this is the most straightforward way to pay for it. But pay for it you will. Rates of $200-$300+ per hour are not uncommon. You are less likely to be cheated, but you still have the challenge of knowing if the advice itself is going to be good or bad for your financial health.

4. Some combination of 1, 2 & 3 from above

This is our last option. If your advisor is using it, likely the reason is not for your benefit.

So what's my advice on picking a good advisor? Beats me. Doing so is probably even more difficult than picking winning stocks or actively managed mutual funds.

Advisors are only as good as the investments they recommend. Since those are mostly actively managed funds—as opposed to the index funds this book suggests—how often do those outperform?

As we saw in Chapter 8, very rarely. You'll recall the research shows ~20% outperform in any given year and looking at a

30-year period that drops to less than 1%. Statistically speaking that's a rounding error; just so much noise.

This is what your highly paid advisor is selling you.

If you are a novice investor you have two choices:

1. You can learn to pick an advisor.
2. You can learn to pick your investments.

Both require effort and time. But the second not only provides better results, it is the easier and less expensive path. Hopefully this book is showing where it lies.

The great irony of successful investing is that simple is cheaper and more profitable. Complicated investments only benefit the people and companies that sell them.

Remember that nobody will care for your money better than you. With less effort than choosing an advisor, you can learn to manage your money yourself, with far less cost and better results.

PART III:

MAGIC BEANS

"Wisdom comes from experience. Experience is often a result of lack of wisdom."

—Terry Pratchett

Chapter 24

Jack Bogle and the bashing of index funds

While no one ever has, if someone were to ask me what single thing has most impeded the growth of my personal wealth the answer would be my stubborn rejection of the concept of indexing for an embarrassingly long number of years. Indeed, when I hear the arguments against it, it is my own voice in my head I hear. I made them all too often and far too long.

So, why is it that the concept of indexing meets with such resistance in some quarters? First, a little background.

Jack Bogle founded the Vanguard Group in 1974. He is the creator of the modern low-cost index fund and my personal hero. If you aspire to be wealthy and financially independent, he should be yours as well.

Before Mr. Bogle, the financial industry was set up almost exclusively to enrich those selling financial products at the expense of their customers. It mostly still is.

Then Mr. Bogle came along and exposed industry stock-picking and advice as worthless at best, harmful at worst and always an expensive drag on the growth of your wealth. Not surprisingly, Wall Street howled in protest and vilified him incessantly.

Mr. Bogle responded by creating the first S&P 500 index fund. The wails and gnashing of teeth continued even as Bogle's new fund went on to prove his theories in the real world.

As the years rolled on and the evidence piled ever higher, Mr. Bogle's critics began to soften their voices; mostly I'd guess because they had begun to sound pretty silly. Other fund companies, realizing that people were becoming ever less willing to accept high fees for questionable performance, even began to offer their own low-cost index funds in an effort to keep their customers from walking out the door. Personally I've never believed their hearts were in it, and for that reason my money stays at Vanguard.

The basic concept behind Vanguard is that an investment firm's interests should be aligned with those of its shareholders. This was a stunning idea at the time and to this day it is the only firm that is, and as such is the only firm I recommend.

The basic concept behind indexing is that, since the odds of selecting stocks that outperform is so very small, better results will be achieved by buying every stock in a given index. This was soundly ridiculed at the time and in some quarters it still is.

But increasingly over the past four decades the truth of Bogle's idea has been repeatedly confirmed. With that confirmation, the amount of money invested in index funds has continued to gain share. Even Warren Buffett, perhaps history's most successful stock-picker, has gone on record as recommending indexing, specifically for his wife's trust once he has passed.

In the Berkshire Hathaway 2013 annual shareholder letter Buffett writes:

"My advice...could not be more simple: Put 10% of the cash in short-term government bonds and 90% in a very low-cost S&P 500 index fund. (I suggest Vanguard's.) I believe the trust's long-term results from this policy will be superior to those attained by most investors – whether pension funds, institutions or individuals – who employ high-fee managers."

So with all this evidence piling up, why then do some still bash the concept? As we saw in Chapter 11, basically it boils down to human greed, psychology and money.

In short, there is too much money to be made and too much weakness in human psychology for actively managed funds and managers to ever go away. In fact, even with the growing acceptance of indexing, there are still about 4,600 equity (stock) mutual funds being offered as of this writing. To put this in perspective, there are only about 3,700 publicly traded U.S. companies for them to invest in. Yes, you read that correctly. As we saw in Part II, there are more stock mutual funds out there than there are stocks for them to buy.

Wall Street is endlessly creating new products and schemes to sell you, even as they systematically and quietly close those that have failed (which serves to make their track record seem better). But make no mistake, the objective is always to line their pockets, not yours.

My advice: Use the index funds and the company Mr. Bogle created and keep what is yours.

CHAPTER 25
WHY I CAN'T PICK WINNING STOCKS AND YOU CAN'T EITHER

Don't feel bad. As we've seen, most professionals can't either.

Indexing vs. active management is always a fascinating debate; at least for us stock geeks with nothing better to do. Over the decades I've been on both sides of it. For a very long time I laughed at the indexers. I made all of the arguments, and then some. After all, if you just avoided the obvious dogs you'd do better than average, right? As we saw in the last chapter, it's not that easy. But in the summer of 1989, I was still convinced I could win this game.

On a flight back from a business trip, I happened to sit next to a guy who worked for an investment research firm. By the time the flight landed he had suggested I should join them and, at my request, had offered three stock tips. I picked one at random and bought it. Over the next several weeks I watched it triple and by the end of that time I had taken a major pay cut to join the firm in a major mid-career change. Who cared about the salary? The real money would be in the information flow.

There I was, surrounded by the exceedingly bright analysts this firm employed. Each focused on one, maybe two industries and within those industries perhaps 6-10 companies and their stocks. More than one had been honored in the trade press as "Analyst of the Year" for their work. These were folks at the top of their game.

They knew each of these industries, and the companies in them, inside and out. They knew the top executives. They knew the middle managers and the front line people. They knew the customers. They knew the suppliers. They knew the receptionists. They spoke to them all weekly. Sometimes daily.

They still didn't get critical information before anyone else (that's insider trading and foolproof, but illegal). But they did know exactly when and how such information would be released. Of course, so did every other competent analyst around the world. Any new information was reflected in the stock price within seconds.

They issued reports for which our institutional investor clients paid dearly. And yet, accurately predicting stock performance remained frustratingly elusive.

If you've worked in a major corporation it is not hard to see why. The CEO and CFO work with internal forecasts created by their teams. The process looks something like this:

Salespeople are required to forecast what their customers will spend. Since these buys are rarely locked in far in advance, and can be cancelled any time, nothing is truly certain. Add to this all the pending business that may or may not come to fruition and basically you are asking the field salesperson to predict the future. Typically they are not clairvoyant. So, of course, they take a guess.

These guesses get passed on to their managers, who are also not clairvoyant, and who now have their own forecasts and decisions to make. Do I take these sales forecasts at face value? Do I adjust them based on knowing Suzy is an optimist and Harry always sees dark clouds? So, of course, they too take a guess and pass it on to the next layer of management.

So it goes until all these guesses on the inherently unknowable future are consolidated into the nicely packaged budget/

forecast binders presented to top management. More often than not, after one look, they'll say: "This is unacceptable. We can't present this forecast to Wall Street. We need more positive results. Go back and revise these numbers." Back down the chain it goes. Maybe multiple times, and each time the numbers get pushed a bit further from reality.

Predicting the future is a dicey proposition for even the most gifted psychics, and they are not burdened with this process.

Suddenly, my enormous stock picking hubris was clear. Somehow reading a few books and 10-K annual reports* was going to give me an edge? Over not only the professional analysts who lived and breathed this stuff all day every day, but also the executives who run the companies in question? I could succeed where they could not?

Suddenly I realized why even rock star fund managers find it almost impossible to best the simple index over time. And why more fortunes have been created brokering trades than making them.

I cringe at the oft-made suggestion that an investor can read a few books on valuing stocks and go on to replicate Buffett's results. Perhaps the best of these is *The Intelligent Investor* written by Warren Buffett's mentor, Benjamin Graham. It is a great book and if stock analysis interests you, by all means take the time to read it.

But remember that when Graham wrote it in 1949, Jack Bogle's first index fund was still 25 years away. Even actively managed mutual funds were few and far between. Analyzing and choosing individual stocks then was a far more necessary and

---

*   A 10-K is the comprehensive summary report of a company's
     performance that must be submitted annually to the Securities and
     Exchange Commission. Typically, the 10-K contains much more detail
     than the annual report.

useful skill. But as early as the 1950s, Mr. Graham was warming to the concept of indexing and by the mid-1970s in interviews was fully embracing its value.

The idea that individuals can readily outperform the market is, to steal a phrase from my dad, horse hockey. Dangerous horse hockey at that.

People have been trying for decades and yet, there is still only one Warren. Think about it this way:

Remember Muhammad Ali? He was the Warren Buffett of boxing in his day. You and I could have followed his training regimen, maybe even engaged Angelo Dundee to show us the ropes. We could have gotten in top shape, done all our homework, learned the "sweet science." And, after all that effort, would you climb in the ring with Joe Frazier or George Foreman or Sonny Liston?

Not me. I'm no Ali. Or Warren. Neither are you. (Unless of course you are, in which case: Thanks for picking up my book!)

Having read the last chapter, you know what Warren Buffett recommends for individual investors: Low-cost, broad-based index funds. Graham, were he still alive, would too.

If you choose to try to best the averages, God Bless and Godspeed. You may well be smarter and more talented than I. You are most certainly likely to be better looking. I'll look for your name along with Warren's in the not-too-distant future.

I extend the same to all those folks I've met in Las Vegas who assure me they have bested the house. I listen, gaze up at the billion dollar casinos and reflect on how many smarter, more talented and better looking people there are than me.

A little humility goes a long way in saving your ass and your cash.

CHAPTER 26

WHY I DON'T LIKE DOLLAR COST AVERAGING

At some point in your life you may find yourself in the happy dilemma of having a large chunk of cash to invest. An inheritance perhaps, or maybe money from the sale of another asset. Whatever the source, investing it all at once will seem a scary thing, as we discussed in Chapter 5.

If the market is in one of its raging bull phases and setting new records each day, it will seem wildly overpriced. If it is plunging, you'll be afraid to invest not knowing how much further the fall will be. You risk wringing your hands waiting for some clarity and, as you know having read this far, that will never come.

The most commonly recommended solution is to "dollar cost average" (DCA) your way slowly into the market. The idea being that should the market tank, you will have spared yourself some pain. I'm not a fan and shortly will explain why, but first let's look at exactly what DCA is.

When you dollar cost average into an investment you take your chunk of money, divide it into equal parts and then invest those parts at specific times over an extended period of time.

Let's suppose you have $120,000 and you want to invest in VTSAX. Now having read this book so far, you know the market is volatile. It can and sometimes does plunge dramatically. And you know therefore that this could happen the day after you invest your $120,000 and, while unlikely, that would make for a very miserable day indeed. So instead of investing all at once you decide to DCA and thus eliminate this risk. Here's how it works.

First you select a time period over which to deploy your $120,000; let's say the next 12 months. Then you divide your money by 12 and each month you invest $10,000. That way, if the market plunges right after your first investment you'll have 11 more investing periods that might be better. Sounds great, right?

Well it does eliminate the risk of investing all at once, but the problem is that it only works as long as the market drops and the average cost of your shares over the 12 month investment period remains below the cost of the shares the day you started. Should the market rise, you'll come out behind. You are trading one risk (the market drops after you buy) with another (the market continues to rise while you DCA, meaning you'll pay more for your shares). So which risk is more likely?

Assuming you were paying attention while reading Parts I & II, you know that the market always goes up but that it is a wild ride. The other thing you know is that it goes up more often than it goes down. Consider that between 1970 and 2013, the market was up 33 out of 43 years. That's 77% of the time.

At this point you are probably beginning to see why I'm not a DCA fan, but let's list the reasons anyway:

1. By dollar cost averaging you are betting that the market will drop, saving yourself some pain. For any given year the odds of this happening are only ~23%.

2. But the market is about 77% more likely to rise, in which case you will have spared yourself some *gain*. With each new invested portion you'll be paying more for your shares.

3. When you DCA you are basically saying the market is too high to invest all at once. In other words, you have strayed into the murky world of market timing. Which, as we've discussed, is a loser's game.

4. DCAing screws with your asset allocation. In the beginning you will be holding an outsized allocation of cash sitting on the sidelines waiting to be deployed. That's OK if that's your allocation strategy. But if not you need to understand that, in choosing to DCA, you've changed your allocation in a deep and fundamental way.

5. When choosing to DCA, you must also choose the time horizon. Since the market tends to rise over time, if you choose a long horizon, say over a year, you increase the risk of paying more for your shares while you are investing. If you choose a shorter period of time, you reduce the value of using DCA in the first place.

6. Finally, once you reach the end of your DCA period and are fully invested, you run the same risk of the market plunging the day after you are done.

What to do instead?

Well, if you've followed the strategies outlined in Part II, you already know whether you are in the wealth accumulation or wealth preservation phase.

If you are in the wealth accumulation phase you are aggressively investing a large percentage of your income each month. In a sense, this regular investing from your income is a form of unavoidable dollar cost averaging and it does serve to smooth the ride. But the big difference is you'll be doing it for many years or even decades to come. And, of course, you don't have the lump sum option.

But you are putting your money to work as soon as you get it in order to have it working for you as long as possible. I'd do the same with any lump sum that came my way.

If you are in the wealth preservation stage, you have an asset allocation that includes bonds to smooth the ride. In this case, invest your lump sum according to your allocation and let that allocation mitigate the risk.

If you are just too nervous to follow this advice and the thought of the market dropping shortly after you invest your money will keep you up at night, go ahead and DCA. It won't be the end of the world.

But it will mean that you've adjusted your investing to your psychology rather than the other way around.

Chapter 27

How to be a stock market guru and get on CNBC

Back in the day, Louis Rukeyser hosted a PBS program called Wall Street Week each Friday evening. Watching it was an end of the week ritual for me.

He'd open with a commentary on the follies and foibles of the previous market week and then turn to a rotating panel of three Wall Street gurus for their take. Two of my favorites were Abby Joseph Cohen, a relentless Bull, and Marty Zweig, who was always "deeply worried about this market."

Each guest was impeccably credentialed and Rukeyser made it a point to deftly schedule those who would each week present opposing views as to the market's condition and direction. Sometimes one would even prove right.

His commentaries, questions and comments were always delivered with a wink, a smile and with great good humor. Tragically, he passed away in 2006 and the current generation of investors is left without his insights and wisdom.

The key thing his program and its parade of guests taught me is that, at any given time, some expert is predicting any possible future that could conceivably happen. Since all bases are covered, someone is bound to be right. When they are, their good luck will be interpreted as wisdom and insight. If their prediction happened to be dramatic enough, it could also lead to fame and fortune.

Every January, Rukeyser would have each of his guests predict the market's high, low and ending point for the year. I forget his exact line, but after the predictions were in he'd say something like, "...with the understanding that even these experts could be wrong, there you have it." And he'd wink into the camera.

Come the following December, he'd salute those who'd come closest and chide the goats. All great fun, if not taken seriously. I'd even indulge in making my own annual predictions but never seriously and never with the idea of using them to get on TV. Even if I turned out to be spot on, mine wouldn't get me interviewed on CNBC. Not dramatic enough. But then, that's not my ambition. If it is yours, however, here's (with my own knowing wink) how:

Step 1: Make a prediction for a huge short-term swing in the market. Up or down doesn't matter. But down is easier and scarier. Scarier will get you more play if you're right.

Step 2: Document the time and date you made it.

Step 3: When it doesn't happen, wait a bit.

Step 4: Repeat Steps 1-3 until one day you're right.

Step 5: Issue Press Release: Market Plunges!!!, just as (insert your name here) recently predicted.

Step 6: Clear your schedule for media interviews.

Step 7: Send me my 15% agent's fee of your new-found wealth.

Be sure not to issue your press release until events prove you right.

Oh, and keep in mind that once your guru status is established, you'll be expected to be able to repeat it. For months—maybe years—everything you say will be noted. Each misstep will be gleefully documented until you slip from view humiliated and discredited. But also rich if you've played your moment in the sun well.

CHAPTER 28

YOU, TOO, CAN BE CONNED

Not too long ago I made an enemy.

She is the widow of an old friend. Before he died, I promised to try to look out for her a bit.

During a conversation she said I made her feel small. She said I made her feel stupid. There were tears. I'm very likely guilty on both counts. I'm not always tactful. But hopefully, I saved her two million dollars.

Her husband died a while back. Over the years, he worked hard and had accumulated the aforementioned wealth. He loved his wife dearly and knew he would very likely leave her a widow. The money was an act of love. He wanted to be sure she would be financially secure.

But he also knew three things that scared him no end:

1. His wife believed in the proverbial "free lunch." That is, she was always open to come-ons. Free cell phones were an example. Every time their cell phone contract expired, the provider offered a "free" cell phone which she proudly grabbed. Somehow she seemed to miss the two year contract it locked them into, over and over again. While small potatoes, it was a bad sign.

2. The world is filled with predators looking for people precisely like her.

3.   Money and this belief in the "free lunch" attracts them like sharks to bloody chum.

It was this topic of the "free lunch" that set me off and brought her to tears. I was trying to gently coax her into appreciating the risk financial predators pose. She is a very bright woman and seemed to understand. But then she said, "Don't worry. I can't be conned."

"With that you have," I said (and by this point my voice, I fear, was raised) "just violated the first rule of not being conned!"

Make no mistake. You *can* be conned. So can I.

Here's one scam I came across many years ago. Fortunately I read about it. In those days, I might well have taken the bait. It went like this:

One day you receive a letter, or maybe these days an email. In it, an investment advisor introduces himself and offers you a stock tip. For example, ABC Corp is going to dramatically rise in price over the next week or two. Don't invest, he cautions, without doing your homework. But his "proprietary metrics" are pointing to this one as a strong buy.

You're no fool, but you decide to maybe keep an eye on it. Just to see. You don't want to miss a good thing. Sure enough, it sharply spikes up. You could have made 50%, 60% or even 100% on your money in a just couple of days. Damn. Then letter #2 arrives.

This one says BCD Corp is poised to take a sharp fall. Our metrics, it says, say short (shorting is a way to sell stock you don't own on a bet it will decline in price) this stock. You are a careful investor. Again you decide to watch and see, although with a keener interest now.

Sure enough, this one collapses as predicted. Had you acted, big profits would have been yours.

Letter #3 arrives. Then #4, #5 and maybe even #6. Each is dead on. The stock rises, or falls, exactly as predicted. Maybe you even took a chance and profited from one or two. By now, it is hard not to be impressed.

Then you get an invitation to dinner at one of your area's finer restaurants. You and a handful of other "executive level investors" are invited to an informal meeting with Mr. Hasn't-Missed-One-Yet. He'll be discussing his proprietary investment metrics and how they've made him rich.

At dinner, Mr. Hasn't-Missed-One-Yet is soft-spoken. He is warm, kind and concerned. He has all the trappings of wealth, but in a tasteful, understated fashion. Charts and graphs are presented. The exact investment approach is unclear; but then it is proprietary. This is to be expected. Oh—and barely mentioned in passing—it just so happens a couple of slots remain open in his latest investment pool. There is certainly no obligation but, of course, "based on our experience" they will be snapped up by tomorrow. So, if you are interested...

Like all magic, it is of course a trick. Can you spot it? If you can, and this is the first you've come across it, you are sharper than I. But don't get cocky. If not this one, another will arrive and fly under your radar. It can happen to you. Fail to understand this and it inevitably will. That's the first rule. Here's the full set:

Rule #1: Everybody can be conned. Certainly stupid people are marks. But so are the exceptionally bright. The moment you start to think that it can't happen to you, you've become a most attractive target. The easiest victims are those that think they are too smart, too knowledgeable to be taken. This means you, bucko.

Rule #2: You are likely to be conned in an area of your expertise. The reason is simple: Targeting and ego. When con men pick a scam they look for people to whom it will naturally appeal. Those are people in the field. People feel secure and safe in those areas they know well. They believe they will be too smart to be caught unawares. Smart people know the areas they don't know and tend to be far more cautious there. Many of Bernie Madoff's victims were financial professionals.

Rule #3: Con men (and women) don't look like con men. This isn't the movies. They're not going to have slouch hats pulled low over their shifty eyes. Successful con men look like the safest, most trustworthy, honest, stable, comforting people imaginable. You won't see them coming. Or rather you will, and you'll be warmly welcoming them.

Rule #4: 99% of what they say will be true. The best, most effective lies are surrounded by truth. Buried in it. The con, the thing that will leave you broke and with a real reason to cry, is carefully hidden. It is deep in the proverbial fine print.

Rule #5: If it looks too good to be true, it is. There is no free lunch. Not ever. Your Mama taught you this. She was right. Listen to your Mama.

With that said, not all cons are clever. An email from a Nigerian stranger offering you, random old you, millions to accept his money transfer should be obvious. Right?

The stranger knocking on your door and offering cut-rate home repairs because "we just happen to be working in the neighborhood" but only if you pay in cash up front, is a con man. You know this. Right?

Those are the kinds of simple cons my friend's wife was thinking about, and she's right. She is much too smart to fall for them. But those aren't what had her husband worried. It is the clever scammers of the world who seek out the smart, the rich and the lonely.

If you have not already done so, have these conversations with your own spouse or partner. Don't leave it to a tactless (although honest) friend of the family like me.

Given the actuarial tables and her good genes, my own wife will likely also outlive me by a couple of decades. Since I handle our investments, we have this conversation on a regular basis. We review what we own and why. Fortunately, she understands the principles and their importance.

As an aside this is one more reason I'm a fan of index funds. I want to leave her with a simple portfolio she can leave on auto-pilot.

So far these discussions haven't led to my making an enemy of her. Yet. I think.

Oh, and here's how Mr. Hasn't-Missed-One-Yet did it:

It is an inverted pyramid. He starts by selecting a very volatile stock and he sends out 1,000 letters. Half predict it will rise and half that it will fall. The 500 that got the correct prediction get letter #2 with a different volatile stock. The 250 that now have two correct predictions get letter #3 and so on. By letter #6 you have 15 or 16 marks who have gotten six letters in a row with your infallibly accurate predictions. Most will be begging by then to be taken.

Part IV:

What to do when you get there

"Money frees you from doing things you dislike. Since I dislike doing nearly everything, money is handy."

—Groucho Marx

Chapter 29

Withdrawal rates: How much can I spend anyway?

4%. Maybe more.

So, you've followed the simple path big three:

- You've avoided debt
- You've spent less than you've earned
- You've invested the surplus

Now you're sitting on your assets and wondering just how much you can spend each year and not run out. This could be stressful, but it really should be fun. You might even be cheeky enough to ask, "What percent of his own assets does Jim spend?" We'll get to that.

You don't have to have read far in the retirement literature to have come across the "4% rule." Unlike most common advice, this one holds up to our beady-eyed scrutiny pretty well, even though it is really very little understood.

Back in 1998, three professors from Trinity University sat down and ran a bunch of numbers. Basically they asked what would happen at various withdrawal percentage rates to various portfolios, each with a different mix of stocks and bonds, over 30 year periods depending on what year the withdrawals were started. They ran their scenarios both adjusting withdrawal levels for inflation and not adjusting the withdrawal. Whew. Then they updated it in 2009.

Out of the scores of options in the study, the financial media seized on just one of these models: The 4% withdrawal rate, 50/50 stock/bond portfolio, adjusted for inflation. Turns out, 96% of the time, at the end of 30 years such a portfolio remained intact. Put another way, there was just a 4% chance of this strategy failing and leaving you destitute in your old age. In fact, it failed in only two of the 55 starting years measured: 1965 and 1966. Other than those two years, not only did it work, many times the remaining money in the portfolio had grown to spectacular levels.

Think about that for a moment.

What that last line means is that in most cases the people owning these portfolios could have taken out 5, 6, 7% per year and done just fine. In fact, if you gave up the inflationary increases and took 7% each year you would have done just fine 85% of the time. Most of the time taking only 4% meant at the end of your days you left buckets of money on the table for your (all too often ungrateful) heirs. Great news, were that your goal. Also great news if you anticipate living on your portfolio for longer than 30 years.

But the financial media believes that most people don't like to think too hard. By reporting the results at 4% they could report on just about a sure thing. Roll it down to 3% and we have as sure a thing as we'll ever see short of death and taxes. And that's giving yourself annual inflation increases.

While 1965 and 1966 were the last and only two years where 4% failed, remember that more recent start years have not yet had their own 30 year measurable runs. My guess is that if you began your own withdrawals in 2007 and the early part of 2008 just prior to the collapse, you will have hit upon two more years in which the 4% plan is destined to fail. You'll want to scale back.

On the other hand, if you started with 4% of your portfolio's value as of the March 2009 bottom, you're very likely golden.

If you are curious, here's an overview of the Trinity Study you can read for yourself:

http://www.onefpa.org/journal/Pages/Portfolio%20Success%20Rates%20Where%20to%20Draw%20the%20Line.aspx

IN SUMMARY:

Withdrawing 3% or less annually is as near a sure bet as anything in this life can be.

- Stray much further out than 7% and your future will include dining on dog food.
- Stocks are critical to a portfolio's survival rate.
- If you absolutely, positively want a sure thing and your yearly inflation raises, keep your withdrawal rate under 4%. And hold 75% stocks/25% bonds.
- Give up those yearly inflation raises and you can push up towards 6% with a 50% stock/50% bond mix.
- In fact, the authors of the study suggest you can withdraw up to 7% as long as you remain alert and flexible. That is, if the market takes a huge dive, cut back on your withdrawals and spending until it recovers.

If you review the study you'll see it has four tables. Tables 1 and 2 look at how various portfolios performed over time and at various withdrawal rates. Tables 3 and 4 tell us how much money remains in the portfolios after the 30 years have passed. The difference between them is that tables 2 and 4 assume the dollar withdrawal amount is adjusted each year to account for inflation. Let's take a look.

Table 1: Retirement Portfolio Success Rates by Withdrawal Rate, Portfolio Composition, and Payout Period

Annualized Withdrawal Rate as a Percentage of Initial Portfolio Value

Payout Period	3%	4%	5%	6%	7%	8%	9%	10%	11%	12%
100% Stocks				Percent success rate						
15 Years	100	100	97	97	94	93	86	80	71	63
20 Years	100	98	97	95	92	86	77	66	55	51
25 Years	100	98	97	93	90	80	67	55	48	40
30 Years	100	98	96	93	87	76	62	51	40	35
75% Stocks/25% Bonds										
15 Years	100	100	100	100	97	94	90	77	66	56
20 Years	100	100	100	97	95	89	74	58	49	43
25 Years	100	100	98	97	92	78	60	52	42	32
30 Years	100	100	98	96	91	69	55	38	29	20
50% Stocks/50% Bonds										
15 Years	100	100	100	100	100	99	93	73	57	46
20 Years	100	100	100	100	98	88	63	46	32	20
25 Years	100	100	100	100	95	67	48	28	18	13
30 Years	100	100	100	98	85	53	27	15	9	5
25% Stocks/75% Bonds										
15 Years	100	100	100	100	100	100	86	53	34	30
20 Years	100	100	100	100	100	68	35	26	22	14
25 Years	100	100	100	100	68	33	25	17	13	10
30 Years	100	100	100	96	38	24	15	9	5	2
100% Bonds										
15 Years	100	100	100	100	100	73	56	44	29	19
20 Years	100	100	100	92	54	49	28	20	14	9
25 Years	100	100	97	58	43	27	18	10	10	8
30 Years	100	100	64	42	24	16	7	2	0	0

Table 2: Retirement Portfolio Success Rates by Withdrawal Rate, Portfolio Composition, and Payout Period in Which Withdrawals Are Adjusted for Inflation

Annualized Withdrawal Rate as a Percentage of Initial Portfolio Value

Payout Period	3%	4%	5%	6%	7%	8%	9%	10%	11%	12%
100% Stocks				Percent success rate						
15 Years	100	100	100	94	86	76	71	64	51	46
20 Years	100	100	92	80	72	65	52	45	38	25
25 Years	100	100	88	75	63	50	42	33	27	17
30 Years	100	98	80	62	55	44	33	27	15	5
75% Stocks/25% Bonds										
15 Years	100	100	100	97	87	77	70	56	47	30
20 Years	100	100	95	80	72	60	49	31	25	11
25 Years	100	100	87	70	58	42	32	20	10	3
30 Years	100	100	82	60	45	35	13	5	0	0
50% Stocks/50% Bonds										
15 Years	100	100	100	99	84	71	61	44	34	21
20 Years	100	100	94	80	63	43	31	23	8	6
25 Years	100	100	83	60	42	23	13	8	7	2
30 Years	100	96	67	51	22	9	0	0	0	0
25% Stocks/75% Bonds										
15 Years	100	100	100	99	77	59	43	34	26	13
20 Years	100	100	82	52	26	14	9	3	0	0
25 Years	100	95	58	32	25	15	8	7	2	2
30 Years	100	80	31	22	7	0	0	0	0	0
100% Bonds										
15 Years	100	100	100	81	54	37	34	27	19	10
20 Years	100	97	65	37	29	28	17	8	2	2
25 Years	100	62	33	23	18	8	8	2	2	0
30 Years	84	35	22	11	2	0	0	0	0	0

Table 3: Median End-of-Period Retirement Portfolio Values Net of Fixed Withdrawals (Assuming Initial Portfolio Value of $1,000)

Annualized Withdrawal Rate as a Percentage of Initial Portfolio Value

Payout Period	3%	4%	5%	6%	7%	8%	9%	10%	11%	12%
100% Stocks				Ending Dollar Amount						
15 Years	4,037	3,634	3,290	2,978	2,564	2,061	1,689	1,378	1,067	563
20 Years	6,893	6,083	5,498	4,640	3,821	2,907	2,059	1,209	610	51
25 Years	10,128	8,466	7,708	6,094	4,321	2,936	1,765	459	0	0
30 Years	17,950	15,610	12,137	9,818	7,752	5,413	2,461	41	0	0
75% Stocks/25% Bonds										
15 Years	3,414	3,086	2,682	2,293	1,937	1,528	1,169	888	623	299
20 Years	5,368	4,594	3,933	3,177	2,665	2,062	1,339	574	0	0
25 Years	8,190	5,724	4,732	3,889	2,913	1,865	500	0	0	0
30 Years	12,765	10,743	8,729	5,210	3,584	2,262	1,424	800	367	105
50% Stocks/50% Bonds										
15 Years	2,668	2,315	2,015	1,705	1,398	1,097	785	470	187	0
20 Years	3,555	3,018	2,329	1,926	1,462	940	420	0	0	0
25 Years	4,689	3,583	2,695	1,953	1,293	624	0	0	0	0
30 Years	8,663	7,100	5,538	2,409	1,190	466	136	16	0	0
25% Stocks/75% Bonds										
15 Years	1,685	1,446	1,208	961	731	499	254	14	0	0
20 Years	2,033	1,665	1,258	882	521	136	0	0	0	0
25 Years	2,638	1,863	1,303	704	130	0	0	0	0	0
30 Years	3,350	2,587	1,816	647	0	0	0	0	0	0
100% Bonds										
15 Years	1,575	1,344	1,102	886	651	420	211	0	0	0
20 Years	1,502	1,188	926	537	132	0	0	0	0	0
25 Years	1,639	1,183	763	41	0	0	0	0	0	0
30 Years	1,664	1,157	670	0	0	0	0	0	0	0

Table 4: Median End-of-Period Portfolio Values for Retirement Portfolios with Inflation-Adjusted Withdrawals (Assuming Initial Portfolio Value of $1,000)

Payout Period	Annualized Withdrawal Rate as a Percentage of Initial Portfolio Value									
	3%	4%	5%	6%	7%	8%	9%	10%	11%	12%
100% Stocks				Ending Dollar Amount						
15 Years	3,832	1,760	3,005	2,458	2,018	1,427	859	483	44	0
20 Years	6,730	5,808	5,095	3,421	1,953	1,215	361	0	0	0
25 Years	8,707	6,304	5,103	2,931	1,683	0	0	0	0	0
30 Years	12,929	10,075	7,244	4,128	1,253	0	0	0	0	0
75% Stocks/25% Bonds										
15 Years	3,139	1,601	2,163	1,773	1,290	943	612	275	0	0
20 Years	4,548	3,733	2,971	2,051	1,231	450	0	0	0	0
25 Years	5,976	4,241	2,878	1,514	383	0	0	0	0	0
30 Years	8,534	5,968	3,554	1,338	0	0	0	0	0	0
50% Stocks/50% Bonds										
15 Years	2,316	1,390	1,535	1,268	889	489	182	0	0	0
20 Years	2,865	2,256	1,667	1,068	469	0	0	0	0	0
25 Years	3,726	2,439	1,453	583	0	0	0	0	0	0
30 Years	4,754	2,971	1,383	9	0	0	0	0	0	0
25% Stocks/75% Bonds										
15 Years	1,596	1,011	777	456	56	0	0	0	0	0
20 Years	1,785	1,196	778	268	0	0	0	0	0	0
25 Years	1,847	941	67	0	0	0	0	0	0	0
30 Years	2,333	633	0	0	0	0	0	0	0	0
100% Bonds										
15 Years	1,325	852	612	303	48	0	0	0	0	0
20 Years	1,058	621	146	0	0	0	0	0	0	0
25 Years	919	102	0	0	0	0	0	0	0	0
30 Years	626	0	0	0	0	0	0	0	0	0

Note: Data for stock returns are monthly total returns to the Standard & Poor's 500 Index, and bond returns are total monthly returns to high-grade corporate bonds. Both sets of returns data are from January 1926 through December 2009 as published in the 2010 *Ibbotson SBBI Classic Yearbook* by Morningstar.

Table 1: (Financial Planning Association, 2010, Table 1: Retirement Portfolio Success Rates by Withdrawal Rate, Portfolio Composition, and Payout Period) **Table 2:** Inflation adjustments were calculated using annual values of the CPI-U as published in the U.S. Bureau of Labor Statistics at www.bis.gov. (Financial Planning Association, 2010, Table 2: Retirement Portfolio Success Rates by Withdrawal Rate, Portfolio Composition, and Payout Period in Which Withdrawals Are Adjusted for Inflation) **Table 3:** (Financial Planning Association, 2010, Table 3: Median End-of-Period Retirement Portfolio Values Net of Fixed Withdrawals–Assuming Initial Portfolio Value of $1,000) **Table 4:** Inflation adjustments were calculated using annual values of the CPI-U as published in the U.S. Bureau of Labor Statistics at www.bis.gov. (Financial Planning Association, 2010, Table 4: Median End-of-Period Portfolio Values for Retirement Portfolios with Inflation-Adjusted Withdrawals–Assuming Initial Portfolio Value of $1,000)

So if you look at Table 1 and at the 50/50 mix with a 4% withdrawal rate, you see you have a 100% chance of your portfolio surviving 30 years.

Table 2 tells you that if you take those same parameters but give yourself inflation raises, your portfolio's chance of survival drops to 96%. Makes sense, no?

Tables 3 and 4 tell us how much money remains in the portfolios after the 30 years have passed and this, to me, is really compelling stuff. Again, Table 3 assumes a straight percentage withdrawal and Table 4 assumes giving yourself inflation raises. Let's take a look at some examples.

Assuming a 4% withdrawal rate on a portfolio with an initial value of $1,000,000, here's what you'd have left (median ending value) after 30 years:

From Table 3 (without inflation adjusted withdrawals)

- 100% stocks = $15,610,000
- 75% stocks/25% bonds = $10,743,000
- 50% stocks/50% bonds= $7,100,000

From Table 4 (with inflation adjusted withdrawals)

- 100% stocks = $10,075,000
- 75% stocks/25% bonds = $5,968,000
- 50% stocks/50% bonds = $2,971,000

This is very powerful stuff and it should give you a lot to feel warm and fuzzy about as you follow *The Simple Path to Wealth*.

As you look over these tables, one thing that should become very clear is just how powerful and necessary stocks are in building and preserving your wealth. This is why they hold center stage in *The Simple Path to Wealth*.

What is likely less obvious—but every bit as important—is the critical importance of using low-cost index funds to build your portfolio. When you start paying 1-2% fees to active mutual fund managers and/or investment advisors all these cheerful assumptions wind up in the trash heap. Wade Pfau, Professor of Retirement Income at the American College for Financial Services and one of the most respected observers of the Trinity Study, says it best:

"For an example of this, the 50-50 portfolio over 30 years with 4% inflation-adjusted withdrawals had a 96% success rate without fees, 84% success rate with 1% fees, and 65% success rate with 2% fees."

In other words, using the Trinity Study projections with portfolios built from anything other than low-cost index funds is invalid.

So, now to answer that question we alluded to earlier: What withdrawal percentage do I personally use in my retirement? I confess I pay so little attention it took a few moments to figure it out and even once I did, it wasn't exact. But my best guess is for the last few years it has run somewhere north of 5%. This casual approach may surprise you. But there are mitigating circumstances:

1. I had a kid in college. That is a huge annual expense, but as of the Spring of 2014, it has gone away. During her college years, the money for it was figured into my net worth, but it was also earmarked as "spent."
2. Since my retirement, my wife and I have accelerated our travels and the related spending has spiked sharply. Not to be morbid, but at my age I am more worried about running out of time than money. If the market were to tank in a major way, this is an easy expense to adjust.
3. Sometime in the next few years we will have two nice new income streams coming online in the form of Social Security.
4. Most importantly, I know I'm well under the 6-7% level that requires close attention.
5. Given the above, going forward my guess is it will drop to under 4%.

Within that 3-7% range, the key to choosing your own rate has less to do with the numbers than with your personal flexibility. If as needed you can readily adjust your living expenses, find work to supplement your passive income and/or are willing and able to comfortably relocate to less expensive places, you will have a far more secure retirement no matter what rate you choose. Happier too I'd guess.

If you are locked into certain income needs, unwilling or unable to ever work again and your roots go too deep to ever seek out greener pastures, you'll need to be much more careful. Personally, I'd work on adjusting those attitudes. But that's just me.

4% is only a guide. Sensible flexibility is what provides security.

CHAPTER 30
HOW DO I PULL MY 4%?

At some point—if you have been following the simple path described in this book—you will be able to choose to have your assets pay the bills rather than your labor.

How quickly you reach this point will have much to do with your savings rate and how much cash flow you require. In any event, your assets will have reached the point where by providing ~4% as discussed in the last chapter, they can cover all your financial needs. Or said another way, your assets now equal 25 times your annual spending.

Having left your employment, you will have rolled any employer-based retirement plans, such as a 401(k), into your IRA and the investments themselves will be split between stocks and bonds held in the allocation that best matches your personal risk profile. Ideally, these will be in Vanguard's low-cost index funds: VTSAX for stocks and VBTLX for bonds.

As we discussed in Chapter 19, these two funds will be in your tax-advantaged and ordinary (taxable) buckets. By this time you will have pared these down to just three: IRA, Roth IRA and taxable. My suggestion—and personal portfolio—is to hold them as follows:

- VBTLX in the IRA, as it is tax-inefficient.
- VTSAX in the Roth IRA, because this is the last money I would spend and the money most likely to be left to my heirs. Roths are an attractive asset to leave upon your death

and, since this is my most long-term money, the growth prospects of VTSAX make it the preferred investment here.
- VTSAX also goes into the taxable account because, of the two funds, it is more tax-efficient.
- VTSAX is also held in our regular IRAs, as even it can benefit from tax-deferral.

As you can see, if you are single you will actually have four fund accounts —VBTLX in your IRA and VTSAX held in all three places: Roth, IRA and taxable. If you are married, your allocation might look something like ours.

I hold:

- VTSAX in my Roth and in my regular IRA.
- Our entire bond allocation in VBTLX in my regular IRA.

My wife holds:

- VTSAX in her Roth and in her regular IRA.

Jointly we hold:

- VTSAX in our taxable account and minimal cash for spending needs in our savings and checking accounts.

So together we have two Roths, two IRAs and one taxable account. Across these we have one investment in VBTLX and five in VTSAX. Our allocation is 75/25, VTSAX/VBTLX.

It is also very possible that, even if you've embraced the simple path in this book, you still have other investments. If these are in your tax-advantaged accounts you've likely rolled them tax-free into Vanguard. But if they are in taxable accounts, the prospect of a hefty capital gains tax might have persuaded you to hold on to them. When I retired, we also had some of these "cats and dogs," mostly in the form of individual stocks I had yet to break the habit of playing with.

At this point the discussion risks becoming a bit complex. There is almost an endless array of ways you might withdraw the ~4% you'll be spending from your investments. So, let's start with the mechanics of how this works and then I'll share with you some guiding principles and exactly what we are doing and why. From there, you should have the tools you need to form your own strategies.

MECHANICS

If you hold your assets with Vanguard, or any similar firm, the mechanics of withdrawing your money could not be easier. With a phone call or a few clicks online, you can instruct them to:

- Transfer a set amount of money from any of your investments on whatever schedule you choose: Weekly, monthly, quarterly or annually.
- Transfer any capital gains distributions and/or dividends and interest as they are paid.
- You can log on their website and transfer money with a few clicks anytime.
- Or any combination of these.

This money can be transferred to your checking account or anywhere else you choose. The process couldn't be much easier and a phone call to Vanguard—and likely most any other firm—will get you friendly and helpful assistance in walking through it all the first time.

Next, let's look at some of the guiding principles behind the approach we use.

First, notice that in constructing our 75/25 allocation, we look at all of our funds *combined*, regardless of where they are held.

Second, we have all our dividends, interest and capital gains distributions in our *tax-advantaged accounts* reinvested. I am not captivated by the idea of "living only off the income" (that is, dividends and interest) as many are. Rather, I look toward drawing the ~4% the research has shown a portfolio like mine can support.

Third, we have the dividend and capital gains distributions from VTSAX in our *taxable account* sent directly to our checking account. Since the payment of these is a taxable event, it makes no sense to reinvest them only to turn around and withdraw the equivalent amount of money shortly thereafter.

Fourth, I want to let my tax-advantaged investments grow tax-deferred as long as possible.

Fifth, as I am within ten years of age 70 1/2, I want to move as much as I can from our regular IRAs to our Roths, consistent with remaining in the 15% tax bracket. You'll recall this strategy from our discussion on RMDs (required minimum distributions) in Chapter 20.

Sixth, once we hit age 70 1/2 and are faced with RMDs, these withdrawals will replace those we had been taking from our taxable account. The taxable account will then be left to grow again.

PULLING THE 4% IN ACTION

1. First, we think about the non-investment income we still have coming in. Even once you are "retired," if you are actively engaged in life you might well also be actively engaged in

things that create some cash flow. We are no longer in a savings mode, but this earned money is what gets spent first. And to the extent it does, it allows us to draw less from our investments and allows them in turn still more time to grow.

2. Remember those "cats & dogs" I had leftover in our taxable accounts? Upon entering retirement, those were the first assets we spent down. We started with the ugliest ones first. While you may or may not choose to follow the rest of our plan, if you have such remnants left in your own portfolio, I strongly suggest this is how you off-load them. Do it slowly, as needed, to minimize the capital gains taxes. Of course, if you have a capital loss in any of them, you can dump them immediately. You can then also sell some of your winners, using this capital loss to offset those gains. You can use up to $3,000 per year of these losses to offset your earned income. Any tax loss you can't use you can carry forward for use in future years.

3. Once those were exhausted, we shifted to drawing on our taxable VTSAX account. We will continue to draw on this account until we reach 70 1/2 and those pesky RMDs.

4. Since the taxable VTSAX account is only a part of our total, the amounts we now withdraw each year far exceed 4% of the amount in it. The key is to look at the withdrawals not in terms of the percent they represent of this one account, but rather in the context of our entire portfolio.

5. We could set up regular transfers from the taxable VTSAX as described above, but we haven't. Instead my wife (who handles all our day-to-day finances) simply logs on to Vanguard

and transfers whatever she needs whenever she notices the checking account getting low.

6. This withdrawal approach may seem a bit haphazard, and I guess it is. But as explained in the last chapter, we don't feel the need to obsess over staying precisely within the 4% rule.

7. Instead, we keep a simple spreadsheet and log in our expenses by category as they occur. This allows us to see where the money is going and to think about where we might cut should the market plunge and the need arise.

8. Each year I calculate what income we have and—consistent with remaining in the 15% tax bracket—I shift as much as I can from our regular IRAs to our Roths. This is in preparation for the RMDs coming at age 70 1/2. When that time comes, I want our regular IRA balances to be as low as possible.

9. Once we reach age 70 1/2, we will stop withdrawing from our taxable account and let it alone again to grow once more. Instead, we will start living on the RMDs that now must be pulled from our IRAs under the threat of a 50% penalty.

10. While I'm fairly certain the money in our taxable account will last until we reach 70 1/2, if it were to run out we'd simply begin drawing money from our IRAs ahead of the RMDs. In essence, this would be the money I had been shifting into the Roths. And, again, I'd strive to keep what we withdrew consistent with staying in the 15% tax bracket.

11. Despite my efforts to lower the amounts in our regular IRAs, the RMDs—once we are both forced to take them—will likely

exceed our spending needs. At this point we will reinvest the excess in VTSAX in our taxable account.

There you have it. While you could, you don't have to follow this exactly. You are free to adapt what works best for your situation and temperament.

For instance, if the idea of touching your principal goes against your grain and you want to spend only what your investments earn, you can instruct your investment firm to:

- Transfer all your dividends, interest and capital gain distributions into your checking account as they are paid.
- Since all these together will likely total less than that ~4% level, should the need arise, you could occasionally log on and simply transfer some more money by instructing that a few shares be sold.
- Or have your dividends, interest and capital gains transferred as they are paid and schedule transfers from your taxable account on a regular basis to bring the total up to ~4%.

For example, if you had $1,000,000 in your portfolio allocated 75/25 stocks and bonds:

- At 4% your withdrawals equal $40,000
- Your $750,000 in VTSAX earns ~2% dividend, or $15,000
- Your $250,000 in VBTLX earns ~3% interest, or $7,500
- That totals $22,500 and if that's all you need, you're done.
- But if you want the full $40,000, the remaining $17,500 you'd withdraw by selling shares from your taxable account. Taken monthly it would be ~$1,500.

This seems overly cumbersome to me and I present it only to illustrate how someone focused on living on only their investment income might approach things.

Here's what I would *not* do

I would *not* set up a 4% annual withdrawal plan and forget about it.

As we saw in the last chapter, the Trinity Study set out to determine how much of a portfolio one could spend over decades and still have it survive. Adjusting each year for inflation, withdrawals of 4% annually were found to have a 96% success rate. This became the 4% *Rule* designed to survive the vast majority of stock downturns so you wouldn't have to worry about market fluctuations in your retirement.

It made for a great academic study and it is heartening that in all but a couple of cases the portfolios survived just fine for 30 years. In fact, most of the time they grew enormously even with the withdrawals taking place.

Setting aside that in a couple of the scenarios this approach would leave you penniless, in the vast majority of cases it produced vast fortunes. Assuming you neither want to be penniless or miss out on enjoying the extra bounty your assets will likely create, you'll want to pay attention as the years roll by.

This is why I think it is nuts to just set up a 4% withdrawal schedule and let it run regardless of what happens in the real world. If markets plunge and cut my portfolio in half, you can bet I'll be adjusting my spending. If I was working and got a 50% salary cut I would, of course, do the same. So would you.

By the same token, in good times I might choose to spend a bit more than 4% knowing the market is climbing and that provides a strong wind at my back.

Either way, once a year I'll reassess. The ideal time is when we are adjusting our asset allocation to stay on track. For us, that's on my wife's birthday or whenever the market has had a 20%+ move, up or down.

True financial security—and enjoying the full potential of your wealth—can only be found in this flexibility. As the winds change, so will my withdrawals. I suggest the same for you.

CHAPTER 31

SOCIAL SECURITY: HOW SECURE AND WHEN TO TAKE IT

Back in the early 1980s I remember railing against Social Security to my mother, who was on it. She'd grown up with the specter of little old ladies living on cat food. That was a real possibility when she was a girl and the elderly were the poorest group in America. I explained to her that if I and my two sisters were let off the SS hook we could not only give her more than her monthly check, we'd have extra left to feather our own nests. She wasn't buying it.

And I wasn't buying it, either. I never figured Social Security would be there for me. All my financial planning has been based on the idea that if it wasn't, no problem. If it was, that would be a pleasant surprise. Well, surprise! Now I'm just a few short years from collecting, and a surprisingly hefty amount at that. Considering what we've paid in and assuming we live long enough, it turns out to be a pretty sweet deal. I hadn't counted on the power of the AARP, the most formidable lobby in history.

Social Security was born in 1935 during the depths of the Great Depression. Those hard times devastated almost everybody, but none more perhaps than the elderly who were no longer able to work even in the unlikely event work might be found. Many were literally living on cat food, if that could be had.

Back in those days, life expectancies were considerably lower. Figuring this can be tricky as the biggest reducer of average life expectancy is deaths in childhood. But if we look at the life expectancies of people who have survived to the age of 20, we get a more useful number. In 1935, for men the average was around 65, for women about 68. Since then, life expectancy in the U.S. has continued to expand. As of 2013, according to the World Health Organization, it is now ~77 for men and ~82 for women.

From those numbers it's easy to see that setting the age to collect Social Security at 65 was a pretty good bet for the system. All workers would pay in, but relatively few would live long enough to collect and those who did would only collect for a few years. This worked so well in fact (with some fairly minor adjustments along the way) that it was only around 2011 that the money flowing in stopped amounting to more than the money being paid out. So well the total surplus reached 2.7 trillion dollars by 2011.

But as you can also see, now the wheel has turned. The huge baby boom generation that has been paying in these surpluses has begun to retire. In addition, they are living a whole lot longer. Going forward, if nothing changes, the system will be paying out more than it takes in. It looks like this:

- 1935-2011: Annual surpluses build and end up totaling about 2.7 trillion.
- 2012-2021: Annual payroll taxes fall short of the annual payouts. But the ~4.4% interest on the 2.7 trillion will cover the gap.
- 2021-2033: The interest payments will no longer be enough to make up the payout difference and we'll start drawing down on the 2.7 trillion.

- 2033: The 2.7 trillion is gone.
- After 2033: The payroll taxes then collected will only be enough to cover 75% of the benefits then scheduled to be paid out.

WHERE EXACTLY IS THIS 2.7 TRILLION?

The 2.7 trillion dollar surplus is commonly referred to as the Trust Fund and it is held in U.S. Treasury Bonds. This as of 2012, by the way, is about 16% of the roughly 16 trillion dollar U.S. debt. In a real sense we owe it to ourselves. In fact, about 29% (4.63 trillion) of our 16 trillion debt is owed to ourselves in this fashion: Social Security, Medicare and the balance in Military and Civil Service Retirement programs. Only 1.1 trillion/8.2% is owed to China, our top foreign creditor and the one we hear most about. We owe Japan about the same. (As of 2016, the total U.S. debt is now over 19 trillion.)

DOES THIS 2.7 TRILLION REALLY EVEN EXIST?

You've probably heard scary talk that this Trust Fund doesn't really exist. That the government has already spent the money. Well, yes and no.

There is no "lock box" somewhere stuffed with $100,000 bills. (These were printed in 1934 and commonly called Gold Certificates. Woodrow Wilson was the portrait on them. They were only used by the government for official transactions between Federal Reserve Banks and were never available to the public.)

The Trust Fund is in a whole bunch of U.S. Treasury Bonds.

To answer the question, "Is the money really there?" you need to understand a bit about what these bonds are and how they work.

Any time any entity sells a bond it is to raise money it intends to spend. The bond and its interest are then paid back with future revenues. As it happens, U.S. Treasury Bonds—what the Trust Fund holds—are considered the safest investments in the world. Backed, as the saying goes, by "the full faith and credit of the United States Government." Of course, that's us, the U.S. taxpayers and the same folks owed most of the 2.7 trillion.

So the U.S. Treasury Bonds held by the Trust Fund are real things with real value, just like the U.S. Treasury Bonds held by the Chinese, the Japanese, numerous bond and money market funds and countless numbers of individual investors.

YEAH, BUT I'D STILL FEEL BETTER IF THEY HADN'T SPENT THE MONEY I CONTRIBUTED AND IF IT REALLY WAS COLD HARD CASH IN A LOCK BOX I COULD DRAW ON.

Well, OK, but cash is a really lousy way to hold money long term. Little by little inflation destroys its spending power.

It is important to understand that any time you invest money, that money gets spent. If you hold a savings account at your local bank, your money isn't just sitting in a vault. The bank has lent it out and is earning interest on it. It is not all instantly available.

If that is an unacceptable risk, your alternative is to stuff your cash in your mattress or a safe deposit box. Had the government done that, the Trust Fund would now be overflowing with currency. That is, pieces of paper money backed by, you guessed it, "the full faith and credit of the United States Government."

At least the Treasury Bonds pay interest.

When should I begin taking the money?

Once you reach age 62, you can begin receiving Social Security. The catch is, the sooner you start, the smaller your checks. The longer you delay (up until age 70), the bigger the checks. Of course, the longer you delay the fewer the years you'll be collecting.

Countless articles have been written about strategies attempting to answer the question as to when to begin receiving benefits. All kinds of fancy, sometimes complex strategies, are described. I've read a bunch and my view is in the end it's really pretty simple: Since the government actuarial tables are as good as they get, the payments are pretty much spot on with the odds. Here's what, in order, you have to ask yourself:

1. When do I need the money? If you genuinely need the money right now, nothing else matters. But each month you delay, your monthly check gets bigger.

2. Do you think Social Security will collapse and stop paying? If you believe this, clearly you'll want to collect while the collecting is good. For what it's worth, I happen to think you're wrong and I'll explain why further on.

3. How long are you going to live? The longer you live, the more advantageous delaying is. The break even point between age 62-66 is around age 84. That is, if you live longer than 84 you will collect more in total by delaying your benefit until past age 66. If you think you'll die before 84, you might want to take the money sooner. Unless...

4. You are married and you were the higher earning spouse. Then you also want to consider how long your spouse will live. If your spouse is likely to outlive you, upon your passing he/she will be able to trade in their lower Social Security payments for your bigger checks.

For example, my wife and I are both in good health. But looking at family histories, and because women usually outlive men, my best guess is that she'll survive me. I figure I'm good to maybe 80-85. Were I alone, I'd start drawing ASAP. But she could easily see 95 or 100. When I die she'll have the option of switching from her benefit to mine. Since mine will be larger, that's what she'll do. To maximize that check for her, I'll delay taking my benefit until I'm 70. She'll start hers at 66.

Another thing worth considering: As we reach advanced age our mental acuity diminishes. Managing our investments becomes harder. We become more reliant on others. At that point, a reliable monthly government check has more value than just the dollars.

Of course there's no way to know what the future really holds. The best we can do is play the odds.

BUT SOCIAL SECURITY IS DOOMED! I'M TAKING MINE ASAP.

There are those who choose to take their benefits the moment they turn 62, even though the amount is reduced. Some simply need the money right now and have no choice. But others are acting out of fear. They believe Social Security will collapse in their lifetime and they want to get what they can while they can. I'm not worried. If you are 55 or older you'll collect every dime. Here's why:

1. Social Security is backed by the most powerful lobby in history: AARP.
2. Geezers are an increasing proportion of the population.
3. Geezers vote.
4. Politicians rarely try to take anything away from a large population that votes.

5. This is why all the possible solutions being suggested thus far affect only those age 55 and under.

WELL THAT'S ALL WELL AND GOOD, BUT I'M UNDER AGE 55! WHAT ABOUT ME?

For anyone 55 and over, Social Security has turned out to be a pretty great deal. But my generation and the generations older than I are likely the last that will enjoy such lofty benefits. The system is in trouble and clearly changes will have to be made. For those under 55 today the deal is likely to be a lot less sweet. You can expect:

1. To get 100% of any promised benefits, but the promises will be smaller.
2. It will cost you more. Income caps (the amount of your income subject to Social Security tax) will continue to be raised. In 2003 the cap was $87,000. In 2013 it was $113,700. That's a trend that will continue.
3. The "full retirement age" will continue to rise. It used to be 65. For me it's 66. For anybody born in 1960 or later it is 67. Those ages will continue to rise.
4. Benefits may become "means tested." That is, based on your need rather than what you paid in.
5. Congress will continue to tinker and in the end Social Security will still be there.

SO, IS SOCIAL SECURITY A GOOD DEAL?

Well, it kinda depends. For the fiscally responsible types reading this book, probably not. If you took that 7.65% of your income you are compelled to contribute, along with the 7.65% your employer is compelled to kick in (as of 2015), and invested it over the decades using the strategies presented here, you'd likely be far, far ahead. Plus your money would be in your hands and not subject to the whims of the government. But that's just the few of us.

I'm realistic enough to know most people are goofs with their money. Without Social Security many would be back to living on cat food. Not only would the rest of us have to read about their sad plight, something much more draconian than Social Security might well be implemented to remedy the situation. So, yes, for most people it will turn out to be a good deal. And probably for society as a whole. But not for you. Or me.

MY RECOMMENDATION

Plan your financial future assuming Social Security will NOT be there for you. Live below your means, invest the surplus, avoid debt and accumulate F-You Money. Be independent, financially and otherwise. If/when Social Security comes through, enjoy.

WANT TO KNOW WHERE YOU PERSONALLY STAND WITH SOCIAL SECURITY RIGHT NOW?

Go here: http://ssa.gov/myaccount/. This is the Social Security website and, once you create an account for yourself, you'll be able to track where you stand. You'll also be able to check and make sure that the record of your earnings is accurate. This is very important as the size of your checks will be in part determined by how much you earned over the years.

CHAPTER 32

HOW TO GIVE LIKE A BILLIONAIRE

I know what you're thinking. For some time now you've been wondering what exactly Mrs. Collins and I have in common with Bill and Melinda Gates. Here it is:

We both have Charitable Foundations

Now you're thinking, "I knew it! Jim is a billionaire!" In this you'd be, sadly I must say, mistaken. More monk than minister, I'm afraid. We don't even have a fancy Gates-like building to house it in.

We've talked a lot about investing and building your own F-You Money, but virtually nothing on, well, spending it. Since we personally don't much care for owning things I've not much to say. We like to travel. We do spend on that. Sending our daughter to college was money well spent, as she so thoroughly embraced the experience.

But the money we've spent that has provided us with the most pure personal pleasure is that we've been privileged to give away.

In fact, I can specifically pinpoint the $1,200 that has given us the most satisfactory return of all. I hesitate telling this story as it will be easy to read it as bragging when it's only meant to illustrate a point. I hope you take it in that spirit.

Many years ago we attended a charitable auction held by the Catholic grammar school our daughter then attended. We had always been impressed with the teachers and the Mother Superior who ran the place.

One of our favorite local restaurants was called Parker's, after the chef who owned it. On this occasion Parker had donated for auction a gourmet dinner for ten. On the spur of the moment we decided to win it and gift it to the school's teachers.

Bidding was spirited but as the amounts reached the actual cost of dinner for ten at Parker's, the competition dropped off. At around $1,200 we were the winners.

When I gifted it to the Mother Superior I also gave her two obligations. First, she would have to choose which ten—of the fifteen total—teachers would get to go. Second, she herself would have to attend. See, we knew this Mother Superior and needed to head off her selfless ways.

When word spread a couple of very interesting things happened. Parker himself stepped up and expanded his donation to dinner for fifteen so everyone got to go. Another bidder offered to foot the bill for the wine.

Well, you know what happens when you mix fine food, wine and Catholic school teachers. Let's just say a good time was had by all, and leave it at that...

In addition to personal pleasure, one of the benefits of charitable giving is the tax deduction. Of course, to gain this benefit you must itemize your deductions on your tax return. For instance, if you are married and filing jointly you are allowed a standard deduction of $12,600 in 2015. Should you have less than that in itemized deductions you are better off taking the standard deduction and saving yourself the effort.

A few years ago it occurred to me that two life changes were coming down the pike that would affect my personal tax situation. We were planning to sell our house and I was planning to retire. Without the house and its associated deductible costs we'd no longer be itemizing. Upon retiring I'd be in a lower tax bracket. Both these things would lower the tax advantage of charitable giving. The solution:

The JJ Collins Charitable Fund

You already know I'm a huge fan of Vanguard. So it should be no surprise that in setting up our foundation we used The Vanguard Charitable Endowment Program. Here's why:

- You don't have to be a billionaire. You can open your own foundation with as little as $25,000. Fancy building not included.
- You get the tax deduction in the year you fund your foundation. So I got to take the tax benefits when they mattered most to me.
- If you have stocks, mutual funds or other assets that have appreciated in value you can move these directly into your charitable foundation. You get the tax deduction for their full market value and you don't have to pay any capital gains taxes on the gain. Double tax win and more money for your charities.
- If you are faced with the RMDs we discussed in Chapter 20, you can roll all or part of a tax-advantaged account directly into your charitable foundation tax free.
- You can choose a variety of investment options so your donation grows tax-free while waiting for you to allocate it.
- You decide which charities receive your money, how much, and when. You can set this up to happen automatically.

- You can add more money to your foundation whenever you choose. (If your balance falls below $15,000 you will be charged an annual $250 Account maintenance fee.)
- Because it is run through Vanguard, expenses are rock bottom.
- Now I can tell unwanted solicitors, "We only give through our foundation. Please send us your written proposal." We've gotten exactly zero proposals.
- It keeps our personal names off the lists some charities sell to other solicitors.

In addition to the tax advantages this offers, it also plays into some of my personal conclusions regarding charitable giving:

- It is best to concentrate your giving. We have selected just two charities.
- Giving small donations to many charities might be satisfying to you, but it dilutes the impact and a greater percent of your gift is eaten up in the processing of it.
- Many small donations also gets you on many mailing lists.
- Never give to phone solicitors.
- The more I see a charity advertising, the less likely I am to believe they are focused on delivering my cash to those they claim to serve.
- You need to do your homework. In addition to scams, many charities simply aren't very efficient in delivering your dollars to those in need.
- Several websites vet charities. This is the one I've used: www.charitynavigator.org

You don't need a charity to help

There is also something to be said for giving outside the traditional, and tax deductible, places. Helping your friends and neighbors directly isn't deductible, but it has immediate benefits all around. This is something I'll be trying to do more of in the coming years, especially since I'm not currently itemizing my deductions.

Finally, while giving is a fine and pleasant thing, no one has an obligation to do so. Anyone who tells you differently is trying to sell you something—most likely the idea of giving to them and/or their pet projects.

As individuals we only have one obligation to society: To ensure we, and our children, are not a burden to others. The rest is our personal choice. Make your own and make the world a far more interesting place.

Afterword

"Everything you want is on the other side of fear."

— Jack Canfield

Chapter 33

My path for my kid: The first 10 years

My daughter recently graduated from college. This is the early life financial path I suggest to her. But you don't have to be just out of college or in your twenties to implement this plan. If you are older and looking to make a change toward wealth, think of it as a ten-year plan.

- Avoid debt. Nothing is worth paying interest to own.

- Avoid fiscally irresponsible people and certainly don't marry one.

- Spend the next decade or so working your ass off building your career and your professional reputation.

- This is not meant to suggest you must be some sort of office drone. Think of your career in the most expansive of terms. The possibilities are endless.

- Take those low-cost college living skills you've honed and use them to pursue any number of new adventures.

- Don't get trapped by an expanding lifestyle or unwind it if you already are.

- Save and invest at least 50% of your income. Put this in VTSAX or one of the other options we've discussed in this book.

- Fund any 401(k)-type employer tax-advantaged plan you are offered.

- Fund your Roth IRA when your earnings and the income taxes on them are low.

- Fund your Traditional IRA once your earnings and the income taxes on them begin to rise.

- Do this for the next ten years or so and you'll be well on your way to financial independence.

- Save more than 50% and you'll get there sooner. Save less and it will take a bit longer.

- If you get lucky with the market you'll get there sooner. If not, it will take a bit longer.

- During this accumulation phase, celebrate market drops. While you are in the wealth accumulation phase, these are gifts. Each dollar you invest will buy you more shares.

- But never fall prey to thinking you (or anyone else) can anticipate or time these drops.

- Sometime in your early to mid-thirties (or 10-15 years after you start) two things will happen: Your career will be hitting its strongest surge and you will be closing in on financial independence.

- Once 4% of your assets can cover your expenses, consider yourself financially independent.

- Put another way, financial independence = 25x your annual expenses.

- That is, if you are living on $20,000 you have reached financial independence with $500,000 invested.

- If, like our friend Mike Tyson used to, you are living on $400,000 a month / $4.8 million a year, you're going to need $120 million.

- As you can see, being financially independent is every bit as much about controlling your needs as it is about building your assets.

- Once you are financially independent, begin living on your investments.

- At the point you become financially independent, you can decide if you are still having fun and want to continue your career or try something new.

- If you keep working, invest 100% of your earnings. You are living on your investments now. This will dramatically accelerate the growth of your assets.

- Note: You don't have to implement these last three points literally. Rather, this is a way to think about your assets and income. Most likely, in executing this concept you will want to spend from your earned income while keeping your investments intact and adding to them.

- This growth of your assets will, in turn, accelerate the growth of the spendable dollar amount 4% represents.

- As long as you are working, VTSAX can serve all your investing needs. The money you add along the way will smooth the ride.

- Once you decide you are done working, diversify into bonds. The more bonds you add, the smoother the ride but the lower the growth.

Once you've reached financial independence and are able to live on 4% of your holdings, should you so choose, now is the time:

- To begin expanding your lifestyle. Just be sure to keep your spending level at 4% of your holdings.

- To think about giving like a billionaire as we discussed in Chapter 32.

- To have children, if you plan to. You are still plenty young enough, financially secure and with financial independence you can arrange your affairs in such a fashion as to give them the time they deserve.

- To consider buying a house, if you are so inclined. But don't be in a hurry. Houses are not investments, they are expensive indulgences. Buy one only when you can easily afford it and if it provides the lifestyle change you want.

You're young, smart, healthy and tough. By your thirties you'll have F-You Money and you should have a blast getting there. Once you've got it, it will continue to expand, as will your personal options. Your future is so bright it hurts my eyes to look at it.

That's what I have told and will continue to tell my daughter.

So, if you are also in college or a few years out and wanted to know what your kindly old Uncle Jim suggests, there you have it. Like everything we've discussed, it is all about expanding your opportunities in life.

If you are a bit more seasoned, don't despair. It's never too late. It took me decades to figure this stuff out. Like mine, your road has likely already had more bumps than those who follow this path from the start will endure. But those bumps are in the past. It is your future that matters and that starts, for all of us, right now.

Chapter 34

Tales from the
South Pacific

One day many years ago I was having an especially bad day at work. Late in the afternoon I called my not-yet-then-but-soon-to-be wife and said:

"I'm sick of this crap. Let's quit our jobs and run away to Tahiti." I'm not entirely sure I knew where Tahiti was at the time.

She said, "Sounds good. I can get a deal on the airfare."

Two weeks later a lovely Tahitian girl was hanging a welcoming lei around my neck and I was learning I'd need to be careful what I suggested around this woman I had proposed to marry.

Muk

Tahiti is a collection of islands in the South Pacific, each seemingly more stunning than the last. On one of these we stayed for a while in a hut built over the crystal clear water.

One morning, lingering over coffee in the outdoor cafe on the grounds, a trim, athletic fellow came up to our table. He was barefoot and shirtless. He introduced himself as Muk, one of the hotel owners. An obvious American by his accent.

Exceedingly curious, of course we invited him to join us. Muk is a great conversationalist and storyteller. He began by confessing he had noticed my not-yet-then wife lounging about the day before and had almost upbraided her for slacking in her duties. She very much looks like a Tahitian.

All very amusing, but not answering my burning question.

"So," I said, "how exactly does a guy from the U.S. wind up owning a hotel in Tahiti?"

Turns out Muk and two of his pals had graduated from university somewhere in Michigan in the early 1960s. From there they moved to California. Casting about for something to do, one of them noticed a small classified ad offering a pineapple plantation for sale in Tahiti. Dirt cheap. Remember, Tahiti had yet to become a famous tourist destination.

They bought it sight unseen and began packing their bags.

I said, "Did you know anything about pineapple growing?"

"Not a thing," said Muk.

"Did you grow up on a farm?"

"Nope. We were all city kids."

"But surely you worked on a farm while going to school?"

"Never even set foot on one."

They get to Tahiti and go to work on their pineapple plantation. Within a couple of months it becomes clear why it was dirt cheap. Turns out you can't actually make a living growing pineapples in Tahiti. Broke and getting broker, stranded in paradise, they began to wonder about their options. That's when the local bank in Papeete invites them to a meeting.

Seems down the hill from the plantation on the water is a half-built hotel. The builder has bellied up and given up. Would Muk and his pals, the bank asks, be willing to finish it? Generous terms, of course.

"Wait a second," I said, "did you guys have any construction experience?"

"Not a bit."

"But you'd run a hotel before then, right?"

"Nope."

"Worked in one?"

"Never. But we had stayed in some occasionally."

"So why in hell, and I mean this in the most pleasant possible way," I said, "would a bank gift a half finished hotel and construction loans to you guys?"

"Their back was against the wall and we were Americans. Americans had a reputation for getting things done."

Muk and his pals lived up to that reputation. Despite their lack of experience, they got the hotel finished and operating profitably. Then they went on to build and operate others, including the one where we stayed.

By the time we met he was rich, barefoot, shirtless and getting richer. Oh, and living in paradise to boot.

By the way, in writing this I got to wondering about Muk and Googled him. Turns out he's now 80 and going strong. Some of his story details are different than I recall and have presented here, but clearly we weren't the only ones upon whom he made an impression.

But Muk was not the only person in Tahiti we met who had managed to put life together on their own terms.

Over dinner

One evening we wandered down the beach to a little place on the sand for dinner. Out in the bay there were several beautiful sailboats.

While we were having drinks, a dingy detached from one of the boats and made its way to shore. A couple about our age (late 20s at the time) got out, walked up the sand and took the table next to us. We got to talking. Soon we were sharing a table and having dinner together. Unfortunately, I have forgotten their names, but I'll never forget their story.

They had sailed over from Los Angeles and were spending four months roaming the South Sea Islands. What, I asked, did they do that allowed for such a thing?

Turns out this guy had two partners and the three of them owned two things together: That sailboat and a business in LA. On a rotating basis, two would be in LA running the business while the third would be out playing with the boat.

Clearly you'd need partners you trusted implicitly, but with that in place this might be the sweetest deal I've come across. These guys, along with Muk, are great examples of living boldly.

While rare, they are not alone. Over the years I've come across any number of people embracing life on their own terms. They are intent on breaking the shackles of debt, consumerism and limiting mindsets, and living free. They are filled with ideas and courage.

This freedom, to me, is the single most valuable thing money can buy and it's why I offer you the strategies in this book.

CHAPTER 35

SOME FINAL THOUGHTS

ON RISK

If you decide to pursue financial freedom you are going to have to choose to spend your money on investments. Somehow in our culture this has come to be seen by most people as deprivation. That has never made much sense to me. Personally, there is nothing I'd rather buy or own than F-You Money.

With it, the world's possibilities are endless and you are faced with the delicious decision as to what to do with your freedom. The only limits are your imagination and your fears.

But while it might not entail deprivation, investing does mean taking on risk.

The investing approach in this book is based on the premise that the stock market always goes up. After all, the Dow Jones Industrial Average started the last century at 68 and ended at 11,497. That was through two world wars, a deflationary depression, bouts of high inflation and countless smaller wars and fiscal disasters. If you want to be a successful investor in this current century, you need some perspective.

Some seek absolute security, but it simply doesn't exist.

Can I be sure the U.S. economy is not about to enter the 25-year down cycle Japan is still living through? Or something worse? Nope.

Is a 4% withdrawal rate always going to be safe? Nope. About 4% of the time it will come up short and you'll need to adjust.

What about asteroids or super volcanos or viruses or alien invaders or an ice age or the reversal of the magnetic poles or AI robots or nanobots or maybe zombies taking us out? Relax. It ain't gonna happen. At least not on our watch.

The Earth's been around for some 4.5 billion years. Multi-celled life has been running around for about half a billion years or so. Major Armageddon extinction events, like the asteroid that took out the dinosaurs some 65 million years ago, have happened about five times. So that's about one every 100 million years or so.

Are we really arrogant enough to think it's going to happen in the geological eye-blink we'll be around? That we'll be the ones to witness it? Not likely.

And if I'm wrong? If any of these life—or even civiliza-tion—ending events take place, how we are invested will matter not a single whit.

This is not to say we face no risks. If you have money you have risk. You don't get to choose not to have risk, you only get to choose what kind. Consider:

- Stocks are considered very risky, and they are certainly volatile in the short term. But go out 5-10 years and the odds strongly favor handsome returns. Go out 20 years and you are virtually guaranteed to be made wealthier in owning them. At least if the last 120 tumultuous years are any guide.
- Cash is considered very safe. But every day its spending power is eroded by inflation. Over a few years, this is no big deal and cash is absolutely where you want to

keep any money you plan to spend in the short-term. But go out 10-20+ years and it is a very big deal—an almost guaranteed loser.

Perhaps it is more useful to think not in terms of risk, but rather volatility. Stocks have far more volatility than cash and in return provide far more wealth-building potential. Cash has little volatility, but you pay for that in the slow erosion of its spending power.

To answer "Which is best?" you must first answer "What are your needs, psychology and goals?"

We all must play the odds and make our decisions based on the alternatives. But in doing so we must also realize that fear and risk are often overblown, and understand that letting our fear control us carries its own set of risks.

Getting past my own fears has allowed me to avoid panic and ride out financial disasters like the one that occurred in 2008. It has given me my own F-You Money. It has allowed me to indulge in my own somewhat risky passions. This book is designed to help you do the same.

Having come this far, you now have a solid understanding of how investing really works and how to realistically build your wealth. You also now understand that the road can be rocky and that plunges in the market are normal. Armed with this knowledge, such events begin to lose their power to create fear in you, allowing you to avoid panic and stay focused on your goal of building wealth and achieving financial freedom.

The Path is before you. You need only take the first step and begin. Enjoy your journey!

"It's rare to find a book that truly changes your life, but JL Collins' common-sense explanations allowed me to see clearly what was previously so muddled. All the stress and indecision I previously felt with investing has melted away and, for the first time, I feel 100% confident in my strategy. I am forever in his debt and have become an evangelist for his approach.

"If you're serious about your financial life, you need to read this book!"

Brad Barrett, CPA
Richmond Savers and Travel Miles 101
www.richmondsavers.com
www.travelmiles101.com

The Simple Path to Wealth provides a refreshingly unique and approachable take on investing. It's not only about reaching financial freedom, it's about building a better life. It's not about finding the next hot thing. It's about sticking to the small number of time-tested principles that actually work and anyone can implement. If you're looking for a way to use your money purposefully and intelligently to create a life you enjoy, this is it."

Matt Becker
Founder, Mom and Dad Money
www.momanddadmoney.com

"This is the 'START HERE' book I recommend to everyone interested in investing. An amazing overview of everything you need to know. This is easily the best foundational investing book available. If you're thinking of investing, this book will radically increase your confidence. If you're already an investor, this book will help you optimize your investing strategy to get better results. These simple principles are astoundingly effective. I followed his guidance and went from zero to a six-figure investment portfolio in less than five years."

Hahna Kane Latonick
Bestselling Author of *Master Your Money:*
Stop Yearning, Start Earning
www.hahnakane.com

"JL Collins is the consummate expert on sane, rational investing methodology and he has a knack for explaining the underpinnings of the stock market in a straightforward, approachable manner. Collins' writing is thorough, informative, and best of all—effective. Most importantly, he's one of the rare financial experts who isn't trying to sell you something or rip you off."

Mrs. Frugalwoods
www.frugalwoods.com

"Hey Millennials, listen up. *The Simple Path to Wealth* is an essential addition to your financial library. Sure, you could probably figure this out on your own, but why reinvent the wheel? It's everything you should've been taught about investing and finances in high school. With funny personal anecdotes and a ton of valuable lessons, you can't afford to not buy this book!"

Gwen
Founder, Fiery Millennials
www.fierymillennials.com

"JL Collins' blog is where I send those wanting to learn about effective investing. Now, in this book, he has managed to take all the confusing investing knowledge of our age, and condense and clarify it into something anyone can understand. Despite the simplicity of the message, the outcome is powerful: the most effective investing strategy one can implement, whether beginner or expert!"

Joe Olson
Adventuring Along
www.adventuringalong.com
Chief Moderator, http://forum.mrmoneymustache.com

"Investing doesn't have to be difficult. In fact, it's much better when it's not and the people who try to make it complicated are often the ones hoping to move your money into their pockets. *The Simple Path to Wealth* contains everything you need to know to become a successful investor so read it, ignore all the other nonsense, and one day you'll have more money than you know what to do with!"

The Mad Fientist
www.madfientist.com

"Personally, I don't follow the strategy laid out in Collins' book. But then, I have spent years of work and study developing and managing my own. For those who don't want to do this, I'd recommend this book. If your goal is financial independence, you're going to need strategies that are optimal for your skills, talents, and temperament. Those in *The Simple Path to Wealth* will serve you well."

Jacob Lund Fisker
Early Retirement Extreme
www.earlyretirementextreme.com

"Jim takes a topic that is often complex and sometimes intimidating, and shares it in way that anybody can understand. Finally there is a book I can recommend that explains how to become wealthy in a way that is both easy to understand and easy to implement."

Jeremy Jacobson
Go Curry Cracker
www.gocurrycracker.com

"Whenever I think about writing anything on investing, I recall JL Collins' insight and logical advice in *The Simple Path to Wealth*, marvel at its brilliance, then dramatically pluck a piece of paper from my typewriter, crumble it in resignation and go learn another recipe from my mom. I cannot improve upon the best."

Anita Dhake
The Power of Thrift
www.thepowerofthrift.com

"JL Collins has the gift of making boring financial concepts funny and interesting. He makes complicated subjects simple and easy to understand. *The Simple Path to Wealth* is the first book I recommend to people curious about financial independence."

Mike Moyer
Mike and Lauren on YouTube
www.mikeandlauren.com

"There are loads of books on investing. This is the one to get. It is smart, thorough and accurate; and sometimes even funny. It is no understatement to say that his principles changed the way I invest and made me wealthier in the process."

Mr. 1500 Days
www.1500days.com

"It doesn't read like an investment advice book, but it gives more bang for the buck than any other investment advice book ever could."

Steve Fallert
Senior Director of Contracts
From one of the Big Five Book Publishers

The Simple Path to Wealth is really about choosing a lifestyle - one that embraces a simple three-step philosophy that will change the way you view life, and how you live it: spend less than you earn, invest wisely, and avoid debt. The book includes simple parables that untangle unnecessary complexity and show how the power of compound interest can provide you with the wealth of freedom. The writing is straightforward and colloquial, and powerful points are highlighted in a way that is easy to grasp. Reading this book can be a wise investment in your future, as well as a clear reminder of what is really important in life."

T. Mullen
Roundwood Press
www.roundwoodpress.com

"Based on JL Collins' excellent blog Stock Series, this book deserves to become a "go to" resource for investors. He cuts through all the spin, complexity and jargon of Wall Street and makes investing simple enough for anyone to manage their own portfolio. Crucially, JL Collins covers the mental and emotional aspects of investing as well as the technical aspects which is rare amongst investment writers."

The Escape Artist
www.theescapeartist.me

"*The Simple Path to Wealth* is the investing book I always wished I'd read. Collins breaks down otherwise-daunting concepts and terminology to make learning the world of investing easy and enticing. He tells you everything you need to know to get started and to continue on with success. This is the only book on wealth and investing that you need to read."

Julie Morgenlender
Founder, Nest Egg Chick
www.juliemorgenlender.com

"Jim enjoys a financially independent lifestyle while sharing money and life lessons through his blog. His Stock Series introduced passive index investing to a wide audience. Now you can get the same wisdom, distilled in book form. Jim tells you how to avoid common investing fears, misperceptions and mistakes. He teaches about diversification, asset classes, asset allocation and the best way to use retirement plans. This is a simple, proven path to investment success from a guy who actually did it. If you're new to investing, don't miss this crash course in the essentials!"

Darrow Kirkpatrick
Retired at 50
www.caniretireyet.com

"As small business owners, our biggest fear is always about how we plan for retirement. Collins removes the mystery and nonsense surrounding investing. We feel much more confident about how we invest our money. We love our business, but love even more that work is becoming a choice, not a requirement."

Jay Dedman and Ryanne Hodson
Scavenger Life
www.scavengerlife.com

"I came of age in the midst of the Great Recession. Like many of my peers, I developed an unhealthy fear of the market. By the time I finally realized investing was one of the best ways to build wealth while beating inflation, I had no idea how to do it. Then I started reading JL Collins. This book makes one of the most overwhelming financial tasks not just simple, but exciting. While time has taught us that the market doesn't always go up in a perpetually straight line, Collins has taught us how to invest so the ups and downs don't hurt so badly. And he's taught us how to do it without getting a headache."

Brynne Conroy
Femme Frugality
www.femmefrugality.com

"A brilliant collection of practical, personal finance advice that produces extraordinary results for your financial happiness. JL Collins has a knack for fact driven investment ideas that you can learn from to strengthen your financial muscle. A masterful must-read for anyone who expects financial peace."

Shilpan
Street Smart Finance
www.streetsmartfinance.org

"This book should be required reading for any new investor! In it you'll find comprehensive investing information, along with some neat tips and interesting twists to help make the most of your money. The JL Collins common-sense approach to building wealth makes it easy for anyone to be successful."

Mindy Jensen
Community Manager
www.biggerpockets.com

CPSIA information can be obtained
at www.ICGtesting.com
Printed in the USA
LVHW031520030222
710035LV00001B/87